HOME SWEET HOME

School

Gentle moments of encouragement for Christian homeschooling mothers

By Nicki Truesdell

www.nickitruesdell.com

Contents

Introduction...1

He who calls you is faithful..3

Dear Mama, go to Jesus...7

There is no greater ministry......................................9

Household staff...11

Crying out to God..13

Setting the tone...15

Training..17

Getting it all done...19

Fear is a liar..21

Use your flexibility for hospitality..........................23

Keeping the HOME at the center of homeschooling....27

Homeschooling with babies and toddlers................31

Homemade Education...33

Revival of domestic religion.....................................35

What is socialization, anyway?................................37

Homeschooling with littles.......................................39

Quiet Time..42

High school content over credits.............................44

Me-time..46

The stages of a homeschooled child.......................49

George Washington's Mother....................................51

Dedicated to my children, who made everything I learned
about homeschooling possible:

Claudia
Chloe
Nicholas
Nathan
Catie

Train them up...52

No greater joy..54

The best curriculum.......................................56

Make the memories now.................................58

Raising teens..60

Rabbit trails...62

What really matters..64

Logic and scripture..66

A formula for family discipleship...................67

Mother..69

Teaching children the Bible............................70

When moms can't handle their kids.................72

Be bold and truthful..74

International Day of the Woman......................76

Psalm 1...78

Well-read...79

When should a child read?..............................80

Education is discipleship.................................81

Suit up for the battle......................................83

Intentional parenting......................................86

Teaching or entertaining?...............................88

Be faithful repositories...................................90

Am I teaching enough?....................................91

5 things about homeschooling that government can't comprehend:93

A long range weapon..94

Interruptions...96

Light a fire..100

Experts vs. moms...101

The made-up science of "levels"....................................103

Do babies crawl on schedule?.......................................104

Creative ways to accomplish your tasks...........................105

Burnout..107

Surrender all...109

Let's talk about curriculum..111

Enjoy the journey..113

Off the beaten path is the best place to be........................114

Scriptures for mothers to pray......................................115

You can (and should) learn with your children....................117

The ministry of motherhood...119

Homeschooling isn't a magic wand..................................121

The lurking danger in the safest small towns.....................123

Public school won't fix disobedience................................125

Be the church...127

Will I mess up my kids?...130

Making memories...131

There's so much more to life than school...........................133

It's okay if you don't have an "Instagram" homeschool..............135

A personalized education...................................137

Dear Ladies...139

The pursuit of Christ....................................141

Resist the urge to run a school..........................143

Creating your own game plan..............................145

Behind, behind, behind...................................147

Teach your children to write well.......................148

There is no such thing as behind.........................149

Managing your home.......................................151

Let go of the world's standards..........................153

Shelter is not a bad word................................155

What qualifies someone to teach a child?.................157

What does homeschooling look like?.......................159

Keep your own schedule...................................161

Cramming or discipling?..................................163

Strength and dignity.....................................165

Whatever you're doing at home is better..................167

"What grade is this book for?"...........................169

Patience, or discipline?.................................171

Flip that schedule.......................................173

Have you tried a year-round school schedule?.............174

Imperfect homeschooling..................................176

Our sacred burden...177

The obedience problem.......................................179

Training is Biblical..181

Titus 2 is for everyone..182

Families are not institutions...............................184

An unspeakable privilege.....................................186

Laura Ingalls Wilder on motherhood....................187

Teaching your children a biblical worldview............189

Training is a marathon..191

Play the long game..193

Physical activity is free.......................................194

Training children for heaven................................196

Don't imitate the world's education.......................197

Bible, reading, and math.....................................199

Does this count?...201

Continue the race..203

Why...204

Dear homeschooling mama,.................................206

References...208

Topical Table of Contents

Academics

- Keeping HOME at the center of homeschooling...............27
- Homemade education...................................33
- Stages of a homeschooled child.......................49
- The "best" curriculum................................56
- Rabbit trails..62
- What really matters..................................64
- Well-read..79
- When should a child read?............................80
- Am I teaching enough?................................91
- 5 things about homeschooling the government can't comprehend..93
- Light a fire...100
- Experts vs. moms.....................................101
- The made up science of "levels".....................103
- Do babies crawl on schedule?........................104
- Let's talk about curriculum.........................111
- You can (and should) learn with your children.......117
- Will I mess up my kids?..............................130
- A personalized education............................137
- The pursuit of Christ...............................141
- Resist the urge to run a school.....................143
- Creating your own game plan.........................144
- Behind, behind, behind..............................145
- Teach your children to write well...................148
- Let go of the world's standards.....................153
- What qualifies someone to teach a child?............157
- Whatever you're doing at home is better.............167
- What grade is *this* book for?......................169
- Families are not institutions.......................184
- Physical activity is free...........................194
- Does this count?....................................201
- Bible, reading, and math............................199

Family discipleship

- Training...17
- A revival of domestic religion..............................35
- Train them up..52
- No greater joy..54
- A formula for family discipleship.......................67
- Psalm 1...78
- Education is discipleship....................................81
- Suit up for the battle...83
- A long range weapon..94
- Dear ladies...139
- The obedience problem......................................179
- Training is biblical..181
- Titus 2 is for everyone......................................182
- Training is a marathon......................................191
- Training children for heaven.............................196
- Don't imitate the world's education...................197
- Why?..204

Motherhood

- He who calls you is faithful..................................3
- Dear Mama, go to Jesus......................................7
- There is no greater ministry.................................9
- Cry out to God..13
- Setting the tone..15
- Fear is a liar..21
- Me-time...46
- George Washington's mother...............................51
- Mother...69
- Surrender all..109
- Enjoy the journey..113
- Scriptures for mothers to pray...........................115
- The ministry of motherhood...............................119
- Shelter is not a bad word...................................155
- Our sacred burden...177

- An unspeakable privilege..186
- Laura Ingalls Wilder on motherhood..........................187
- Continue the race..203
- Dear homeschooling mama.......................................206

Babies and Toddlers

- Homeschooling with babies and toddlers....................31
- Keeping little ones busy..39

Teens

- High school content over credits.............................44
- Raising teens...60
- Cramming or discipling?..163

Culture

- Intentional parenting..86
- Teaching or entertaining...88
- Be faithful repositories...90
- Homeschooling isn't a magic wand............................121
- The lurking danger in the safest small town.................123
- Be the church...127
- Playing the long game...193

Worldview

- Logic and scripture..66
- Teaching children the Bible......................................70
- When moms can't handle their kids...........................72
- Be bold and truthful...74
- International Day of the Woman.................................76
- Teaching your children a Biblical worldview.................189

Homemaking

- Household staff..11
- Getting it all done..19
- Use your flexibility for hospitality.............................23

Daily life

- Quiet time……………………………………………………………42
- Stages of a homeschooled child………………………………49
- Make the memories now……………………………………………58
- Interruptions……………………………………………………………95
- Creative ways to accomplish your tasks…………………105
- Bunout……………………………………………………………………107
- Off the beaten path is the best place to be………………114
- Public school won't fix disobedience…………………125
- There's more to life than school………………………………133
- It's okay if you don't have an Instagram homeschool……135
- There is no such thing as behind………………………………149
- Managing your home…………………………………………………151
- What does homeschooling look like?…………………………159
- Keep your own schedule……………………………………………161
- Strength and dignity………………………………………………165
- Patience, or discipline?……………………………………………171
- Flip that schedule……………………………………………………173
- Have you tried a year round school schedule?……………174
- Imperfect homeschooling…………………………………………176

Introduction

When you need a boost of encouragement and only have a few minutes, this book is here for you.

Home educating mothers have a huge responsibility and not enough hours in the day. And if they have a tight schedule or lots of littles, it can be hard to fit in some encouraging reading. That's what I hope to alleviate with this book.

It's patterned after *Keep a Quiet Heart* by Elisabeth Elliot. She collected a series of previously-written articles into one handy place. I have turned to the short, one-or-two page chapters of that book many times over the years. When I wanted a dose of encouragement and wisdom, I knew I could gain that in less than 10 minutes of reading. I could even read the chapters out of order, and it didn't matter; they still blessed my day.

That's what I want to do here: encourage, inspire, and even convict. I want to remind you of the eternal importance of what you're doing, share some of the wisdom that I have been given over the years, throw in a few helpful hints, and nudge you with conviction. Some of this content was previously shared on my social media, some is from my blog, and plenty of it is brand new for this book. Sprinkled throughout, you'll find an encouraging word from some of the people who have encouraged me over the years.

Now, in the spirit of short doses of writing, that's it for the introduction!

Nicki Truesdell

He who calls you is faithful

With every day that goes by, I am more convinced that our call as Christian parents is imperative to the coming generations. We no longer live in the world that we grew up in.

Sin is paraded in front of us and our children in the form of love and tolerance. We can't avoid it. It's in the grocery store, at the park, at school, in children's books, and in children's entertainment. Children who should still be playing childish games are discussing their sexuality with your children on social media, on the playground, at school, and in the neighborhood.

The validity of scripture is no longer even questioned in the world around us. It's treated with hostility and derision. Everywhere your kids turn they are being told that the Bible is outdated, bigoted, hateful, and just plain wrong. The creation account in Genesis is seen as a laughingstock, and it's not just at liberal universities. It's in all levels of public education, children's books and movies, and sadly, some churches.

Are you equipping your children? Are you equipped, yourself? Does it feel overwhelming?

It can feel that way if we let it. Or we can suit up for the battle (Ephesians 6: 10-18) before us and take our roles as protectors seriously. We can defend our gates and train up future soldiers to lead in the coming generations.

Parenting is so much more than food and clothes and shelter and birthday parties. We need to look beyond the material and physical. We have an enormous privilege to raise children who will one day change the world. Will they do it for the better? Will they make a difference? How do we get them there?

Discipleship.

And that only happens when you are the primary influence on your children. Personal relationships with your children are where the real-life education happens.

Be fully engaged. Set aside the time. Suit up for the battle.

Now concerning the times and the seasons, brothers, you have no need to have anything written to you. For you yourselves are fully aware that the day of the Lord will come like a thief in the night.

While people are saying, "There is peace and security," then sudden destruction will come upon them as labor pains come upon a pregnant woman, and they will not escape. But you are not in darkness, brothers, for that day to surprise you like a thief. For you are all children^j of light, children of the day. We are not of the night or of the darkness. So then let us not sleep, as others do, but let us keep awake and be sober. For those who sleep, sleep at night, and those who get drunk, are drunk at night. But since we belong to the day, let us be sober, having put on the breastplate of faith and love, and for a helmet the hope of salvation.

For God has not destined us for wrath, but to obtain salvation through our Lord Jesus Christ, who died for us so that whether we are awake or asleep we might live with him. Therefore encourage one another and build one another up, just as you are doing.

We ask you, brothers, to respect those who labor among you and are over you in the Lord and admonish you, and to esteem them very highly in love because of their work. Be at peace among yourselves. And we urge you, brothers, admonish the idle, encourage the fainthearted, help the weak, be patient with them all. See that no one repays anyone evil for evil, but always seek to do good to one another and to everyone.

Rejoice always, pray without ceasing, give thanks in all circumstances; for this is the will of God in Christ Jesus for you. Do not quench the Spirit. Do not despise prophecies, but test everything; hold fast what is good. Abstain from every form of evil.

Now may the God of peace himself sanctify you completely, and may your whole spirit and soul and body be kept blameless at the coming of our Lord Jesus Christ. He who calls you is faithful; he will surely do it.

(1 Thessalonians 5:1-24)

Dear Mama, go to Jesus

Have you had those moments when you're suddenly overwhelmed? On top of that, you still have children to care for, so what do you do? A shocking phone call, bad news, frustration, sick children…these can put us into a place where we just want to ditch the homeschool day, lock ourselves in the bathroom, and cry.

But often, that's not possible. Our children need us. There's very little time for "mom time out."

Instead of allowing a problem to grow, tackle it head-on. Don't allow yourself to take it out on the children. As you probably already know, this only exacerbates a bad situation.

Dear mamas, go to Jesus.

Pray. Right where you are. If you can't even escape to the bathroom for privacy, just start praying. He hears you. "Cast all your cares on Him, for He cares for you." (1 Peter 5:7) Give Him your sadness, your anger, your disappointment, and your helplessness. Ask for peace. Ask for provision. Ask for wisdom. Intercede for a friend or family member. Keep praying until the negative emotions subside.

Next, if your day cannot continue as usual, reset it. Organize something for the children to do, whether it's a snack and a movie, outdoor play, or quiet reading. Set them up to be occupied for a time. If you really have to, buckle them all in the car and go for a drive.

Now, turn to your Bible. Find comfort in the Psalms. Read it aloud if you can. Let the Holy Spirit wash over you with these soothing words.

This, too, shall pass.

There is no greater ministry

There is no ministry, vocation, career, calling, or cause for a woman to devote her life to that is greater than motherhood.

Too often I've heard mothers claim that their ministry is something other than the children in their home, or that their career is important for their self-esteem, or that they work for a cause that serves the greater good.

Putting our children in the care of others in order to serve others (or self) is saying that God did not know what He did when He created mothers.

The hand that rocks the cradle truly does rule the world. The daily tasks that make up child rearing are the ones that shape the future. The mother has the power to influence several little hearts in her care, and in turn, to influence generations to come.

It feels mundane many days. It feels like you are not as important or fashionable or smart as those other women. That's okay. You are right where God intended when He created you as female.

And while you are busy shaping the future through the little boys and girls in your home, He is allowing you to be shaped, as well.

Household staff

Do your children have regular household chores? And what I mean by that is: do they help with the housework, meals, lawn care, and laundry?

If not, I really want to encourage you to change this. When parents don't give their kids regular chores, it is usually for one of two reasons: needing to control the process and the outcome for perfection, or feeling guilty for making their kids work.

Mamas, I encourage you to let both of these go. Let's explore why.

I know that training kids to do big projects can be messy and can certainly try your patience. I'll admit, it often results in the job taking twice as long and being messier than it should be. But hey: they're kids! Doesn't everything turn out this way?

Do it anyway, and just prepare for the inevitable. When you begin to train children in chores, allow for more time. It *will* take longer in the beginning, but with your patience and their repetition, it will get faster and better.

And then one day you will look up and realize that your son is cooking a complete meal for the entire family, and it's not terribly messy, and it tastes delicious!

Ask me how I know.

Are you one of the moms that feels a little guilty for giving your kids regular work?

Crying out to God

Do you feel like crying some days?

Sometimes the amount of physical and emotional demands on a mother can bring us to tears, especially when a lack of sleep is part of the equation. I have been there. From the earliest days with my first baby, into the teen years with my youngest kids, I have had those days.

Sometimes we fall into the false belief that if we didn't homeschool, our days would be easier. But parenting is hard work, no matter where your kids are educated. Whether you have babies who won't sleep, toddlers who scream, 10-year-olds who won't do math, siblings who argue over silly stuff, or teens who want to be independent from you, parenting is just hard sometimes.

But it's also the most important job there is.

Here's what I can tell you: these seasons are short, and they will pass. You can probably look back on a previous time that was so hard and seemed to last forever, and now it's behind you. That's how it works!

Tears are not a sign of failure. They are a sign of your humanity. They remind you that you need God.

It is of the Lord's mercies that we are not consumed, because His compassions fail not. They are new every morning. Great is Thy faithfulness. (Lamentations 3:22-23 KJV)

Go ahead and let the tears flow for a few minutes. And while you're crying, cry out to God. He is there. He knows your needs.

And then reset your morning, or your day. Pray for and pray with your children. Set the example of trust in God. Turn on some hymns or worship music and sing together. Have a snack. Rock the baby. Have sandwiches for dinner, and serve them with a smile.

Setting the tone

If your mornings feel like a train wreck sometimes, might I suggest planning ahead to create an atmosphere of peace and joy?

The quickest and easiest way to do this is by playing beautiful music as the children are waking up and beginning their day. No matter how many children you have, or their ages, or their neediness, you can do this. It only takes a minute.

We do this a few different ways: hymns, worship songs, and even upbeat happy music. I like to change it up, but not so much that the kids don't have a chance to learn the songs well.

Just think for a moment about how music affects humans. It evokes strong feelings, and it also cements memories. When the music glorifies God, our spirits do the same.

The great hymns of the church have some rich theology in their verses, and when you and your children hear them over and over, that theology does its work.

I am so thankful that my parents did this when they became Christians. I am old enough to have the 1970's and 80's Maranatha Praise! songs still in my head. Not only are these songs a great comfort to me now, but they bring back sweet memories of peaceful mornings in our home.

Training

Training is something that takes an extended period of time. We know that our children must be trained in many behaviors, but we often expect quick results. Mamas, don't get discouraged when you seem to repeat the same thing over and over...you are not alone!

Think about when *you* are trying to break a bad habit or form a new one. It takes time. It takes accountability. You have to be consistent with yourself.

It's the same with raising children. *Consistency* and *time* are more effective than anything else.

So, when it's time to do some training, follow this simple formula:

- Announce.
- Model.
- Implement.
- Repeat.
- Smile.
- Reward.

Pretend you're training a newly hired employee for a job. You don't just expect them to read your mind and know what to do, do you? Treat your child as if they are in training for a new job (whether it's a behavior, certain words, or actions). Tell them what is expected, show them how, start the process, and repeat as necessary (and trust me, it will be necessary!). Give each reminder with a smile, and go through the process again if needed. All along the way, reward them with a "high five," a hug, or a "good job!"

If all of your children are small, or if all of your children are out of control, this may feel impossible at first. Trust me, it is not impossible, and it is well worth your effort. You will look back someday and be glad you took the time.

Getting it all done

How do homeschool moms get it all done? How do we cook, clean, manage, and educate?

Well, sometimes we just don't.

Let's be honest.

Some days we accomplish the longest list of tasks, and other days we barely keep the kids fed. Some weeks are the perfect homeschool weeks, and others are more of an unplanned break from lessons.

And if it doesn't go according to plan, we melt under a load of guilt. Because we are daily treated to the prettiest social media images of moms who craft sourdough bread from scratch while leading their children on a nature hike through the woods, or smiling families of 10 sitting around the school table learning Greek and Latin.

It can be overwhelming.

Just remember that those families are not your family. Remember that we all put our best images on social media. Remember that in homeschooling, there isn't one right way.

You are a family. You are not a school. Family life looks a little different every single day. Roll with it!

Fear is a liar

And it is everywhere.

I am always amazed at the honest statements I hear from moms who are afraid of one thing or another...

...fear that their kids won't match up to the rest of the world...

...fear that their kids will grow up to hate them...

...fear that their kids will turn away from God in adulthood...

...fear of what others will think of the family's choices...

Yet God has told his people *not* to fear over and over again in His word.

Fear not, for I am with you; be not dismayed, for I am your God; I will strengthen you, I will help you,

I will uphold you with my righteous right hand.
(Isaiah 41:10)

Therefore, I tell you, do not be anxious about your life, what you will eat or what you will drink, nor about your body, what you will put on. Is not life more than food, and the body more than clothing? Look at the birds of the air: they neither sow nor reap nor gather into barns, and yet your heavenly Father feeds them. Are you not of more value than they? And which of you by being anxious can add a single hour to his span of life? And why are you anxious about clothing? Consider the lilies of the field, how they grow: they neither toil nor spin, yet I tell you, even Solomon in all his glory was not arrayed like one of these. (Matthew 6:25-34)

Peace I leave with you; my peace I give to you. Not as the world gives do I give to you. Let not your hearts be troubled, neither let them be afraid. (John 14:27)

Do not be anxious about tomorrow, for tomorrow will be anxious for itself. Sufficient for the day is its own trouble. (Matthew 6:34)

Use your flexibility for hospitality

Homeschoolers often overlook the ways in which they can be used for everyday ministry. When a mother and her children are at home, they often have the freedom to adjust their schedule as they see fit.

So, how can this be used for ministry?

Whether randomly, or regularly, a mother and her children have the ability to serve extended family members, fellow church members, and the community at large with their time. We have often been able to drop everything and go serve someone in need *because* we homeschool.

However, I've also seen (and been on the receiving end of) responses to the tune of, "We are not available because we have too much schoolwork to do," or "We are scheduled up all week with co-op and other activities. Sorry!" While I understand trying to stay on schedule, and providing lots of great opportunities for our kids, it saddens me to see real needs going unmet in exchange for school books or activities.

This may be stepping on some toes. I totally get that. But I've felt the conviction of these words, too. I've been too busy before and was not able to make the time to help someone in need.

Dear moms, let's take a hard look at what our priorities are. Do they line up with the scriptures?

But as for you, teach what accords with sound[j] doctrine. Older men are to be sober-minded, dignified, self-controlled, sound in faith, in love, and in steadfastness. Older women likewise are to be reverent in behavior, not slanderers or slaves to much wine. They are to teach what is good, and so train the young women to love their husbands and children, to be self-controlled, pure, working at home, kind, and submissive to their own husbands, that the word of God may not be reviled. Likewise, urge the younger men to be self-controlled. Show yourself in all respects to be a model of good works, and in your teaching show integrity, dignity, and sound speech that cannot be condemned, so that an opponent may be put to shame, having nothing evil to say about us. (Titus 2:1-8)

She opens her hand to the poor and reaches out her hands to the needy. (Proverbs 31:20)

If we are overly concerned about school schedules or high school transcripts, we might very well be focused more on worldly standards.

It's important to consider what message this is sending to our children. We teach by our words *and* by our example. If our schedule is too tight with activities that only benefit us, we eventually train our children that this is acceptable.

But if we show them that our plans can be changed for someone else when needed, they learn at a young age to deny themselves for the sake of others.

Before you schedule up every day of your week with important homeschool activities, consider some ways that you can keep your schedule open to serve when needed. Be ready to take a meal to a new mom or a sick friend (and let the kids help you cook it!). Babysit for a mom who needs help once in a while; your older children can help with little ones, or your younger ones can enjoy a day of playing with them.

I promise you: your children will not suffer from a lack of multiple activities. And I also promise you they will have a full heart from learning to serve others with their time.

Keeping the HOME at the center of homeschooling

I am the product of 1980's homeschooling. In those days, we stayed home all the time because we feared questioning or arrest. (My parents did get arrested the very first month of homeschooling, so we were very careful from that point on.)

Home was the center of our lives. We spent our days a lot like Laura Ingalls Wilder wrote in her original autobiography:

> *"And so, with work and play and music and reading and sleeping, the days and nights passed busily and happily."*

We were not part of any co-op or classes because there was no such thing. So, what did we do?

Meals were all eaten at the family table. We entertained ourselves at home (without a TV, no less!), and went to church every Sunday and

Wednesday. Our parents were our primary influence.

We were not rushed or stressed. Oh, we got up at a certain time every day, did chores, and started school first thing. But, as you may already know, homeschooling doesn't take many hours, so we finished up by early afternoon.

In our free time, we were sometimes bored. And that boredom led to pursuing hobbies and interests, and playing outside with no agenda, or reading our favorite books for hours. We learned to sew, help in the garden, and raise animals. We didn't show the animals or sell our goods. We simply ate the produce and just enjoyed the simple pleasures that they provided.

We had time to talk and laugh and eat together with our parents. Even though my dad had long work days, and sometimes worked multiple jobs, we were almost always at home when he was.

And there was always time for family Bible reading. It was rarely missed because we were not in a hurry to be somewhere.

Mamas, do you find that free time, or family meals, or Bible reading get sacrificed for "good opportunities?" Now that I am grown, with my own children, and have experienced the world of homeschool co-ops and various activities, I can tell you that the benefits they offer don't compare to the slow pace of home life.

Now, you may be thinking we never do classes or activities. We do. But I have learned through trial and error to choose wisely and minimally. We typically only attend our local co-op, which is 20 weeks per year. Occasionally there is an outside class that we will join, but it is rare.

I have found that not only are you busy on the day these classes happen, but there is often an added homework requirement (dictating the time you do have at home), missed naps for littles, laundry piling up, and quite possibly too much fast food because mom is too exhausted to make meals. It's not always worth it in the end.

So, if a great opportunity presents itself (or multiple opportunities), count the cost in advance. Weigh the pros and cons. If it's a class that would really benefit your kids or lighten your academic load, it might be a great fit. Maybe there's an activity that's fun and includes the whole family. These are the best kind!

But if you wind up playing the role of bus driver, homework shuffler, uniform washer, and fee payer, and you are not the primary influence on your children, it might be time to reevaluate.

Homeschooling with babies and toddlers

When you're trying to homeschool with toddlers and babies in the house, it seems like you're fighting an uphill battle. I can't tell you how many moms have asked me, "How do you get school done?" I've even been asked about sending those littles to preschool or setting them up with online preschool curriculum.

Might I suggest a different train of thought?

Your older kids do need an education, and your younger ones need *you*. Try to find a balance between the two. This might involve some drastic changes to your schedule.

Start the morning with focus on the littles— song, stories, even outdoor play.

Then focus on school time. Train your littles to *understand* school time. Teach them to play quietly. Stop school if their behavior is out of control and deal with it right then. Give your school-aged student some independent work to fall back on while you deal with urgent issues.

Teach all of the children how to adapt to interruptions without losing focus. Teach the school children to continue working. Don't allow them to run off and play without your permission. Don't allow the littles to wreck the house while you're doing school.

All of this takes time, dedication, training, and discipline, for you *and* for the kids. Don't expect results in one week. And don't give up.

Parenting is all-in. People say that it's a marathon and not a sprint. That is so true! And training children in self-control, obedience, patience, and independence are just some of the few very important parts of parenting. They need these alongside, before, during, and after academics.

Let academics have their place, but don't put them above time with your littles, or a peaceful home, or child-training.

Homemade Education

Modern parenting has become somewhat like a fast food drive-through. "I'd like to order the standard education, please, with a side of physical activity, a Sunday School class, and top it off with some music lessons."

We want to choose from a menu that's quick and easy and gets the job done. It may fill up the bellies, but does it satisfy? There used to be a common saying in homeschooling, that "we are not merely filling buckets, but we are lighting a fire." I usually say that we are not checking off lists, but educating a well-rounded individual.

What tastes better, is more enjoyable, and is more satisfying? A fast-food burger and fries, or a home-cooked meal with all the trimmings? The drive-through is a simpler option, but the results are very costly to our health. A home-cooked meal takes more of your time, but it's also healthier and more satisfying.

Choosing quality ingredients, taking the time to simmer and bake, adding in interesting side dishes, and gathering around the table together is a feast for the belly and the soul.

The same is true of education at home. There are numerous options, for every budget and every taste. Choose well. Put on your apron and make the healthy meal. Pour your heart into these little people you are raising. Give them a feast!

I know it's more work, it's more tiring, and sometimes it's just plain harder. But isn't that true of everything worthwhile?

Think about this next time you rush to the drive through for burgers and scarf them down in the car, and compare it to when you make a nice meal and eat together unhurriedly at the table.

Spread the feast!

Revival of domestic religion

"We deeply want a revival of domestic religion. The Christian family was the bulwark of godliness in the days of the Puritans; but in these evil times hundreds of families of so-called Christians have no Family Worship, no restraint upon growing sons, and no wholesome instruction or discipline. How can we hope to see the kingdom of our Lord advance when His own disciples do not teach His Gospel to their own children?"

-Charles Spurgeon

Christian homeschooling parents have to remember that homeschooling in itself is not the goal. The goal is to disciple our children. We do this through consistent instruction in the scriptures.

Don't assume they will gain the instruction they need simply by going to church, or by being homeschooled. They need you, teaching them how to read their Bibles, how to see the world from a biblical worldview, and how to think God's thoughts.

What is socialization, anyway?

Next time you wonder about socialization, or when someone quizzes you on how your homeschooled children will socialize, think about what socialization actually is:

- Making eye contact while conversing
- Shaking hands firmly
- Carrying on coherent conversation
- Speaking in complete sentences
- Introducing themselves and others
- Initiating conversation
- Communicating easily with all ages
- Showing interest in others
- Giving up their seat to others
- Inviting a newcomer to join a group
- Avoiding crude language
- Offering company something to drink
- Playing with small children
- Learning not to monopolize a situation

What socialization is not:
- Standing in line
- Sitting in a classroom

- Spending all day with people in your age group
- Bullying
- Peer pressure

What the Bible says: *He who walks with wise men will be wise, but the companion of fools will be destroyed.* (Proverbs 13:20 NKJV)

Homeschooling with littles

Homeschooling small children (and homeschooling *with* small children) can feel like a frenzy. The younger the child, the needier they are. It's just natural. They rely heavily on their mothers for almost everything. But no matter how dedicated you are to the roles of motherhood and home educator, it can still be exhausting.

One of the most common cries for help from homeschool moms is about keeping little ones busy while teaching school-aged children. This can seem impossible, but I promise you: it's not. It just takes some strategy.

I have noticed (and I'm not the only one) that the youngest children just need to know they are loved, noticed, and important. And do you know how they know this? Time. *Your* time.

So, start your school day with time for the little ones. Let them be first, whether it's a family time that includes them, or focused time just for toddlers. If you have independent older children, they might go ahead and get started on their school work while you begin toddler time.

So, what do you do with the toddlers?

There are many easy and meaningful activities. Read a children's Bible aloud, sing a song (with hand motions!), teach them to memorize a short Bible verse, read a picture book, take a walk, push them on the swing, or train them in an easy household chore. You can accomplish so much, even with their short attention spans!

Consistency is key. Thirty minutes at the beginning of each school day is a small chunk of your day, but it makes such a big difference in the tiny world of a toddler.

This accomplishes a few things. Your toddlers get their "mom-love tank" filled up, which usually keeps them happy for a couple of hours. You don't have to think about "mom guilt" because you are deliberately loving on and teaching even the littlest members of the family. And just a few short minutes of reading, singing, and Bible each day go a long way toward their future education!

One more thing: as part of this morning routine, gently remind the littles what you will allow or require them to do next. Whether they are to play quietly with toys, watch a video, sit at the school table with you, or nap, speak plainly and repeat it daily. They *will* learn the routine. You *will* notice the difference!

Charlotte Mason said, *"The mother who takes pains to endow her children with good habits secures for herself smooth and easy days."*[i]

Quiet Time

If you do not have a specific quiet hour in your day, let me encourage you to try. No matter the ages of your children, it can be such a peaceful blessing.

I first implemented this many years ago on the advice of other older homeschool moms. At the time, I had two little boys and two elementary aged girls. After just a few weeks, everyone knew what to expect, and it became a normal, expected part of our day.

For us, quiet time came right after lunch. The little ones who were still napping would go to their beds, and the older kids could choose a quiet place to look at books or do something that didn't involve talking or noise. The one exception was soft music or an audiobook. Each child was in a separate room whenever possible, sitting on their bed, or a couch, or my bed.

This quiet time allowed me to nap if I wanted to, or to accomplish something important without interruption. Quiet time after lunch is also nice calm before storm that often comes when you're trying to make dinner.

If you're unsure how to implement this in your home, start small. Begin with 20 or 30 minutes for the first week, and increase it after that. Encourage your children to make a list of "quiet activities" that they will look forward to. My girls would read, paint their nails, knit or crochet, or even work on school work. My boys would color or draw, play with quiet toys on their bed, and sometimes fall asleep.

When all of my kids passed the age of naps and quiet time (by the time the youngest was about 10), we all kind of missed it.

High school content over credits

Homeschool mamas, don't get caught up in high school credits. Teach your children the really important things *because* they are the really important things.

There are so many things that a young adult needs to know that may not fit perfectly on a high school transcript. You need to teach them things that their future college may not care about.

Teach them anyway.

Teach the Bible, first and foremost. Read it with and to your children.

Educate them in worldview studies. This is so profoundly important, over math and science and composition and history. And yet, it influences all of these.

Give them plenty of time and opportunity to practice critical thinking, debate, and logic.

Train them to be godly men and women, prepared to raise the next generation of godly men and women. How often do we train our offspring for their careers and trades, but teach them very little about the most important role of parenting?

Academics are necessary to a well-rounded individual. Transcripts *are* important. Being well-educated is extremely important for Christians in this world. But education is not just about checking off boxes and creating a snazzy transcript.

Education is shaping individuals. It is molding minds for great things. It is preparing them for whatever path God takes them down, not just the approval of the college admissions board.

Let God's wisdom guide you as a high school counselor, not the wisdom of this world. Check off boxes where appropriate and necessary, but make sure those boxes are not your master.

This life is about so much more than a transcript.

Me-time

Those words are the hope and joy of exhausted mothers, and have become the American Way.

But, oh how unbiblical this mindset is. It's not just self-centered, it is *unbiblical.*

There is rest and peace to be found in the midst of stress, in the midst of noise, in the midst of chaos. The peace that passes all understanding is available to you anytime, anywhere, whether you sit alone on your back porch or in a room full of needy children with toys strewn everywhere.

Now may the Lord of peace himself give you peace at all times in every way. The Lord be with you all. (2 Thessalonians 3:16)

Me-time elevates self. But Jesus has already called us to DIE to ourselves. This is tough. It's unpopular. It's often unpleasant.

I appeal to you therefore, brothers, by the mercies of God, to present your bodies as a living sacrifice, holy and acceptable to God, which is your spiritual worship. (Romans 12:1)

So many mothers have bought the lie that raising children is so hard that they need to get away from it regularly, hire it out, or get the kids off to school. Dear mamas, that is most definitely a lie. God would not give you children if you were not created for the role of motherhood. And you were. Every bit of it.

Denying ourselves is a very spiritual exercise. *And he said to all, "If anyone would come after me, let him deny himself and take up his cross daily and follow me.* (Luke 9:22) It takes discipline, prayer, and meditation on scripture. And it is necessary for the very basic and profound role of motherhood. Because while some days are very basic, others are very profound. You want to be there for all of them.

Trust me, there is no pedicure session or gym class or even ladies Bible study group that will do more for your well-being than the simple, daily exercise of dying to yourself, taking up your cross, wiping little noses, filling sippy cups, settling squabbles, reading the same picture book 1,000 times, cooking endless pots of macaroni and cheese, and following Him. (Matthew 16:24)

So do as Susannah Wesley did in her daily life of raising 19 children...pull your apron up over your face in the middle of a roomful of children, and pray. (In case you don't know, this is the great lady who raised Charles and John Wesley, those great preachers of the 18th century.)

And before you angrily slam this book shut, just know I like lunch with friends, and naps, and pedicures, and there is nothing inherently sinful about these activities. And lunch with friends who point you to Christ can be such a blessing! But these things do not make me a better person. Only a relationship with Jesus, especially through the hardest times, can do that.

The stages of a homeschooled child

1. "Ooh Mommy! I want to do school!"
2. "This is so cool! May I get more books at the library about it?!?"
3. "Why do I have to learn this, anyway?!"
4. "Tell me more about [previously boring topic].

It's not exact, but this is what I've seen in our home: excitement (preschool-ish), enthusiasm (elementary), negativity (middle and high school), and then true interest (also middle and high school, or maybe even after graduation). #3 may be affected by age or by a certain subject (*cough, cough* long division). #4 is the best, when you get to have mature conversations with your teen.

So don't be alarmed when you hit stage 3. Just keep going. And be realistic. There are some "school-ish" things in our curriculum that kids don't really need to do. Be willing to make executive decisions, and stand firm on the important things.

What stages have you observed in your homeschool family?

George Washington's Mother

"GEORGE WASHINGTON was born in the county of Fairfax, Virginia, on the 22nd of February, 1732. He lost his father at an early age, and to the wisdom of his mother he declared himself indebted for the correct formation of his youthful mind.

Matrons of America, if the mother of Washington moulded *his* mind with such beauty and greatness, how much may *you* do to perpetuate, through your sons [and daughters], the prosperity and happiness of your favoured country!

Train their youthful minds in wisdom's ways; guide them in the paths of virtue and patriotism; teach them to love their country and its liberty; and to prize, dearer than life, the sacred boon of freedom that was nobly won and sacredly transmitted by the sages and patriots of '76."

(Able and Mighty Men – Biographies of the Men Who Signed the Declaration of Independence)[ii]

Train them up

"Train them to realize the power of sin. I name this in order to guard you against unscriptural expectations. You must not expect your children's minds to be a sheet of pure white paper which have no trouble if you only use right means. I warn you plainly, you will find no such thing. It is painful to see how much corruption and evil is in a young child's heart and how soon it begins to bear fruit. You must be prepared to see violent tempers, self-will, pride, envy, sullenness, passion, idleness, selfishness, deceit, cunning, falsehood, or hypocrisy. Even in your own flesh and blood, a terrible aptness to learn what is bad, a painful slowness to learn what is good, and a readiness to pretend anything in order to gain their own ends become evident.

In little ways, these sins will creep out at a very early age; it is almost startling to observe how naturally they seem to spring up. Children require no schooling to learn to sin. But you must not be discouraged and cast down by what you see. You must not think it a strange and unusual thing that little hearts can be so full of sin. It is the only portion that our father Adam left us; it is that fallen nature with which we come into the world; it is that inheritance which belongs to us all.

Let it rather make you more diligent in using every means that seems most likely, by God's blessing, to counteract the mischief. Let it make you more and more careful, as much as you are able, to keep your children out of the way of temptation."

J. C. Ryle on *The Duties of Parents*[iii]

No greater joy

"I have no greater joy than to know that my children walk in truth." 3 John 1:4 (KJV)

Before they can walk in the Truth, they must know the Truth. This is our most important responsibility as parents.

Parenting is more than just feeding and clothing. Those are the no-brainers. The important things are what we teach (or fail to teach) our children through our daily conversation and example.

With deliberate and consistent discipleship, we can teach our children to know the Truth, love the Truth, and walk in the Truth. But it takes dedication and discipline on our own parts. It takes up our time.

Deuteronomy 6 teaches us that parents are to teach their children about God all throughout the day, in natural conversation..."when you lie down, when you rise up, when you sit in your house, and when you walk by the way..."

Talk to them about everything. About faith and belief, about the inspired and infallible word of God, about creation, about purity and modesty, about marriage and family, about charity and evangelism.

Point them to the authority of the scriptures and the blessings that result from following God's perfect plan. It is a heavy responsibility but also an incredible privilege to raise up the next generation.

The best curriculum

"What is the best curriculum for [insert] grade?"

It doesn't exist.

Peruse a homeschool convention hall and you'll discover that the options are truly endless. If you've never been to a convention, you may only think there are a few choices, and that most of them are online.

You'd be *amazed.*

Whether you're teaching first grade or twelfth grade, there is no "best curriculum." There is a best one for your family, but it may be different than the best one for your friend.

Because there are *so many* to choose from, it pays to take your time and research.

The beauty of homeschooling is in its individuality. Each homeschool is different than the rest. Each child is unique, and has the potential to be shaped uniquely.

Don't just buy the most-recommended curriculum. Do a little digging to find out if it's truly a good fit for you.

- Ask a few friends
- Search online
- Peruse a used book sale
- Order some catalogs
- Go to a homeschool convention

The best curriculum is the one that suits your family's time, budget, and learning expectations. *That* is the best one for your child.

Make the memories now

"The days are long, but the years are short."

"Motherhood is a marathon, not a sprint."

"It's over before you know it."

As a mom of adults now, I can tell you that all of this is absolutely true. And those years that seemed so hard? I'd give anything to be back there again: diapers, sippy cups, toys everywhere, and sleepless nights.

I don't say this to guilt young moms. I just want to echo what your grandmothers and your mothers and those ladies at church already tell you: enjoy it while it lasts.

How do you enjoy crying babies and Legos all over the floor? How do you enjoy sibling squabbles and piles of laundry?

Maybe enjoy is a strong word.

Relish these days. Take lots and lots of photos. Take lots of videos of them playing and talking and laughing and even crying. Don't toss every drawing and coloring page. Keep a journal if you can make the time.

Today, I have plenty of time to pray and read my Bible without interruption, to read multiple books, to exercise daily, to cook a meal *and* clean the kitchen, to make quilts, to keep the house clean, paint my nails, and run a home business.

And I fondly remember those disorderly, noisy, and messy years.

Don't get me wrong: I'm thankful for the slower days and a quiet home. I will not complain. But I wish I had been more thankful for my chaotic and messy home with many small children so many years ago.

Make those memories now, and be patient for the times to come.

Rejoice always, pray without ceasing, give thanks in all circumstances; for this is the will of God in Christ Jesus for you. (1 Thessalonians 5:16-17)

Raising teens

The teen years are hard.

You know it. You remember. Physical changes, hormones, friends, social situations — they all contribute to making this part of childhood kind of rocky.

Can I just say that *not* being in school really softens the blow of the teen years? I can attest to this for two reasons: I was a homeschooled teenager, and my mom and my husband were not. The comparisons we can make are incredible.

Don't get me wrong: the teen years are hard no matter where you are educated. But being at home with loving parents is a thousand times better than being in the social cesspool of a high school when your face breaks out like never before, or you suddenly feel like crying all day and you don't even know why, or you know you're not one of the "in" crowd.

If you went to a public or private high school, you know exactly what I'm talking about.

Now imagine that you did not have to experience any of that. I didn't. When the teen years came, I had the security of home and family all day every day. I still had acne, I still had raging emotions, I still got nervous around boys; but it wasn't the majority of my day, and it didn't rule my thoughts.

And social pressure? It was very minimal. My friends were from church. My influences were my parents. My heroes were characters in the books I read. And our days were always bathed in scripture.

Take it from me. High school is the best time to homeschool!

Rabbit trails

Some of the best school days we have are the ones where we end up following rabbit trails based on something we discussed in our lessons. We will put aside the lesson plan because the kids asked questions that needed answering. These discussions are probably my favorite part of homeschooling. They aren't on the lesson plan; there's no worksheet or quiz. But these are the times when kids are thinking. They are the ones asking the questions. They are actively involved in their education.

When cultural topics arise, or scientific questions, or inquiries about political happenings, it's such a privilege to be there to point them to the truth. I cannot stress this enough. The social climate in which we live today is toxic. It is anti-biblical. It's not just a blessing to be able to guide my children in their biblical worldview; it is imperative that I do so. When we worked our way from the Civil War to the rise of fascism, you can imagine the topics that came up in this time span! Slavery, civil rights, feminism, evolution, capitalism, communism, nationalism— it's really amazing.

You can't plan this. There's no teacher script for it. And that's probably why homeschooling is so scary.

What if they ask questions you can't answer? What if you don't remember that part of your education?? Who's going to dissect the frog???

And if your child doesn't initiate these conversations? Be patient. Carefully guide them. Encourage discussion and debate, even if they disagree with you. Keep trying. Because there *will* be a topic that gets their attention enough to pull them out of that shell.

Don't fear it. Embrace it. Be willing to say, "I don't know; let's find out together." Be willing to have debates and disagree. But by all means, be there. Be the most influential person in your child's life.

What really matters

Things that don't matter:

- whether they write letters from bottom-up or top-down
- whether they learn times tables in 3rd grade or 6th grade
- whether they learn Latin or not
- whether they take all the classes and play all the sports
- whether they ace the SAT

What does matter:
- that they know how to read
- that they know how to write
- that they know how to compute
- that they know how to learn
- that they love the Lord their God with all their heart, mind, and strength and love their neighbor as themselves

I remember when my oldest girls were young, and I worried about insignificant things.

Things I was told were really important.

Things that kept me thinking I would mess the girls up.

Things that made me push the girls too hard.

Let me tell ya...now that those girls are grown, I know what's important and what's not.

Just the basics. That's all everyone really needs.

The extras are individual choices. They are nice to have. Some adults need those extras. Some don't.

Don't try to force your kids into a standard box. Kids aren't standard. Humans are all unique. Start with the basics and tailor your homeschool around your own family, not everyone else's.

Logic and scripture

We attended an event with Christian astrophysicist Dr. Jason Lisle several years ago, and an audience member asked Dr. Lisle, "What resources do you recommend for young people and college students today for defending their faith and the Scriptures?"

His answer was simple:

1. *The Bible.* Know it intimately. Read it. Study it. Memorize it.
2. *Logic.* Knowing how to think logically is the key to understanding fallacies and knowing how to combat them.

It's not surprising to see that these two very important components are missing in most schools today.

A formula for family discipleship

"But as for you, speak the things which are proper for sound doctrine:

That the older men be sober, reverent, temperate, sound in faith, in love, in patience;

The older women, likewise, that they be reverent in behavior, not slanderers, not given to much wine, teachers of good things—

That they admonish the young women to love their husbands, to love their children, to be discreet, chaste, homemakers, good, obedient to their husbands, that the word of God may not be blasphemed.

Likewise, exhort the young men to be sober-minded, in all things showing yourself to a pattern of good works; incorruptibility, sound speech that cannot be condemned, that one who is an opponent may be ashamed, having nothing evil to say of you."

Titus 2: 1-8

He who walks with wise men shall be wise, but a companion of fools will be destroyed. (Proverbs 13:20)

Training up a child in the way he should go. (Proverbs 22:6)

Teaching God's law to our children when we lie down, when we sit up, when we are at home, and as we walk along the road. (Deuteronomy 6)

Teaching young men to have self-control. (Titus 2:6)

Teaching our children to love their enemies, to pray for their enemies, and to turn the other cheek. (Matthew 5)

Everything we need for instruction in righteousness is in the Bible. Let's put it to work in our homes.

Mother

"But when a little child in a mother's bosom is loved, nursed, caressed, held close to her heart, prayed over, wept over, talked with, for days, weeks, months, years, it is no mere fancy to say that the mother's life has indeed passed into the child's soul.

What it becomes is determined by what the mother is. The early years settle what its character will be, and these are the mother's years."

-JR Miller[iv]

Teaching children the Bible

"Knowledge of the Bible never comes by intuition. It can only be obtained by diligent, regular, daily, attentive reading."
~ J.C. Ryle.

Start with a children's picture Bible or story Bible when your kids are young.

Give your children their own Bible when they learn to read on their own.

Study the Bible with them regularly. Read through the entire Bible together. Teach them how to study the Bible on their own.

Teach them to study topics, books of the Bible, and to use a concordance.

Listen to songs that help commit scriptures to memory.

"...from childhood you have known the Holy Scriptures, which are able to make you wise for

salvation through faith which is in Christ Jesus. All Scripture is given by inspiration of God, and is profitable for doctrine, for reproof, for correction, for instruction in righteousness, that the man of God may be complete, thoroughly equipped for every good work." (2 Timothy 3: 15-17 NKJV)

When moms can't handle their kids

You've probably seen what I've seen. Jokes from moms that can't handle being around their kids all day. They can't wait to get back to their jobs. They can't drink enough coffee or consume enough wine to make it through each day.

I've been told these things in person. By parents, in front of their own kids. It's all over social media. And guess what? A lot of those kids are on social media. They hear the snide comments. They see the memes, too.

I cringe when I read these posts. And I realize that too many parents don't have a generational vision. They don't agree that children are a blessing.

The school is their daycare. They *need* the school to raise their children because they have absolutely no desire to do so.

We shouldn't be shocked that the death rate from abortions is over 60 million since Roe vs.

Wade, when even Christian mothers laugh about how annoying children are.

Children aren't pets, to be fed and bathed and dressed before we head off to our "real" lives. They are the future. They are people. They have needs that no one can meet like a loving mother can.

We are witnessing a sickening truth: that many mothers don't really want to be home with their children all day.

I pray hearts are convicted and changed. I pray that children will become treasured members of their own families. I pray that a revival sweeps this nation and that parents will seek a "new normal" that puts possessions and careers on a back burner for the sake of their families.

As homeschooling mothers, we can set this powerful example. Not by having perfect lives, but by showing with our actions and our words that our children truly are a blessing.

Be bold and truthful

Evolutionary ideas pervade our culture, and we cannot afford to ignore it. We should teach our children to think critically, evaluating assumptions and arguments for and against evolution. As Ken Ham states, "Evolutionary ideas should be taught—but warts and all. There are many inconsistencies within the evolutionary framework and many disagreements about how to interpret the evidence. When appropriate, point out that many scientists, both creationists and evolutionists, do not believe that Darwinian evolution is adequate for explaining the existence of life on earth."

Our approach toward teaching our children ought to be filled with truth of God's Word first, then incrementally identifying and refuting false ideas.

In short, parents should not be intimidated by "the science of evolution" or its proponents. As the Proverbs say, *"The fear of man lays a snare, but whoever trusts in the Lord is safe."* (Proverbs 29:25).

Adherence to God's Word does not require blind faith as belief in evolution does. The God of the Bible is faithful, and His Word is sure. We should make every effort to encourage our children to fear the Lord and greatly delight in His commandments (Psalm 112:1).

International Day of the Woman

Every year there is an International Day of the Woman. I've heard a lot of "inspiration" on radio, TV, and internet on these days, both lamenting the fact that there aren't enough women in typical male industries, and urging girls and women to take those roles.

Don't fall into this form of secular feminism.

Women were uniquely created to do what men cannot do. We are created physically, mentally, and emotionally perfect for our role in this world, and men need us to be just that: perfectly female.

When God created Eve, He said that He would give Adam a help meet for him. (Meet: adjective; *precisely adapted to a particular situation, need, or circumstance : very proper*).

The world doesn't need women who are trying to fulfill two roles. The world doesn't need "equal" women. The world, our country, our homes need women to fulfill their role to the utmost. It's not the lesser role: it's a complementary role.

Ladies, embrace your feminine role. Thank God for the special gifts you have. You will find all the fulfillment you need in being a woman!

Psalm 1

Blessed is the man who walks not in the counsel of the ungodly, not stands in the way of sinners, nor sits in the seat of the scornful. His delight is in the law of the Lord and in this law he meditates day and night. He will be like a tree planted by the rivers of water that bring forth fruit in due season. His leaf shall not wither, and whatever he does will prosper.

The ungodly are not so, but are like the chaff which the wind drives away. Therefore, the ungodly shall not stand in the judgement, nor sinners in the congregation of the righteous. For the Lord knows the way of the righteous, but the way of the ungodly shall perish. (NKJV)

This was the first memorization project we did when my parents began homeschooling us in 1983. We memorized a chapter of the Bible each month.

There's so much more to education.

Well-read

A complete education does not include "selected text" or regurgitations of classic works. Too many are told what a book says, or given snippets of a book as their "education."

Read the whole book.

Read the writings of Goerge Washington, Karl Marx, Adolf Hitler, Thomas Jefferson, Nicola Machiavelli, Martin Luther, Isaac Newton, and others. Read the words of world-changers, all of them. Require it from your high schoolers.

A well-educated population is a free population. Don't just educate your kids enough to get by, to get a job, or to get a college degree. Educate them to think critically.

Educate them for excellence. Educate them to change the world.

The fear of the LORD is the beginning of knowledge; fools despise wisdom and instruction. (Proverbs 1:7)

When should a child read?

"To learn to read and to like it takes about thirty contact hours under the right circumstances, sometimes a few more, sometimes a few less. It's a fairly easy skill for anyone to pick up if good reasons to do so are provided.

You should be with the attitude that NOTHING IS WRONG in the natural variation which finds one child reading at five and another at twelve. By the time both are fifteen nobody can tell which one learned to read first. The pedagogical apparatus which compels age-graded five-year-olds to be ranked according to ability to respond "correctly" to a teacher's urgencies gives rise to our familiar reading pathologies. By the time a seemingly slow reader approaches adulthood, he or she will display indifference to reading, or hatred of it, because of our schools."

-John Taylor Gatto, Weapons of Mass Instruction[v]

Education is discipleship

"...when education itself is understood to be a form of discipleship, and we recognize that a student becomes like his teacher when he is fully trained (Luke 6:40), a great deal of clarity is given to this issue. Education is not simply about imparting facts; it's also about imparting a worldview. And imparting a worldview is not an insignificant endeavor; it is the very act of discipleship. This is ultimately the greatest impetus for reconsidering, rather than assuming, how our children are to be educated." (Josh Niemi, Expository Parenting)[vi]

I say this all the time: homeschooling is not so much about school, but about raising our children full time, with our focus on biblical discipleship.

Sure, we do all the school subjects, play sports with friends, go to classes outside the home, and even learn to play instruments, but the overarching goal is the discipleship of our children. The Christian home is the center of our children's world, not a government school.

And the difference is astounding.

Suit up for the battle

It's so easy to romanticize the old days, hundreds of years ago, when men and boys fought dangerous battles to defend home and country. They seemed to have a glorious purpose that is lacking in our modern world.

King Alfred of Wessex and his men spent their entire lives fighting the Vikings that harassed the English countryside. On land and on sea, up rivers and through towns, these pagan invaders sought to steal, kill, and destroy. The men of Wessex and other British kingdoms knew no other life.

We in the West do not face these dangers anymore. Soldiers may face them in other lands, by choice, but our safety is relatively guaranteed here in the States.

Or is it?

We may not fight with swords and cannons. But we face a far greater and eternal danger: principalities, powers, the rulers of the darkness of this world, and spiritual wickedness in high places. (Ephesians 6:12)

It is visible in the world around us as sexual perversion, suicide, rebellion, atheism, and blasphemy. Our children are surrounded by this spiritual wickedness on every side.

Our sons and our daughters must be protected from this very grave danger. Just as the Vikings in the Middle Ages, our enemy comes to kill, steal, and destroy. He is very real, and battle against him must be waged continuously.

Moms, we have a sword, and it is the word of God. It is our battle plan. It does not change, and it is powerful. Use it daily. Do not be afraid of the enemy.

King Alfred not only led his own men into battle after bloody battle, he did so with an illness that kept him sickly for many years (and which took his life early). He not only defended his land; he sought to convert the pagan enemy to Christianity, and he was successful. He is not called Alfred *the Great* for nothing.

Let us bravely accept our mission as parents. Let us not waver when it's too hard or circumstances distract us. Let us train our children with the same mindset. There is an enemy, and he is dangerous. Our purpose is also glorious: to defend home and family, and to convert the pagans to Christianity. (Matthew 28:19)

Intentional parenting

"Don't let the world raise your children. Be intentional and fill their hearts and minds with the Word of God." (Nancy Leigh DeMoss)[vii]

Intentional parenting is hard. It's the kind of parenting that forces you to think beyond meals and clothes and baths and toys. It means thinking about the hearts and minds of your children, and about God's commands for raising them.

It means stopping what you're doing to remind them of family rules and to give consequences when needed. It means guarding their hearts from worldly influences, even when every friend they have is allowed to partake of those influences. It means talking to them and listening to them. It means *so much more* than meals and clothes and baths and toys.

This is why it's so hard. Because it forces parents to be selfless and aware all the time. But deliberate, consistent training will reap rewards that are uncounted.

Remember, "*he who walks with wise men shall be wise, but a companion of fools will be destroyed,*" (Proverbs 13:20) and God instructs parents to teach our children "*as we sit in our house, and as we walk by the way, and as we lie down, and as we rise up,*" (Deuteronomy 6:6-9).

These things cannot happen when we let the world raise our children.

Teaching or entertaining?

I know it's highly popular to use apps and computer programs for early learning, but they are not necessary, and they can be a problem. There are very few learning games that actually teach. Rather, they *entertain* with educational material. Your student will not be behind by skipping computer games and apps entirely. In fact, focusing more on real books and papers will give them an advantage.

Not only are these games not really educational, they are very juvenile. They do not teach children to appreciate beautiful language or beauty in art or music. They specialize in goofiness, annoying sounds, and dumbed-down dialogue. If Charlotte Mason were alive in the 21st century, she would certainly call these games "twaddle."

Instead, surround your child with things that inspire them to think and create and play. Building blocks of all kinds, art supplies, picture books, and outdoor play will give young children a

well-rounded day that includes mental and
physical stimulation.

Be faithful repositories

"Both man and woman have their own parts to play in bringing faith to the next generation, and the woman's role is particularly important. How can we ever think that the female sex is inferior when we see the essential responsibility God has given women in this world? Their sensitivity to spiritual concerns seems to be far more innate and natural than a man's.

Mothers and wives often are the medium for our intercourse with the heavenly world, the faithful repositories of spiritual knowledge and wisdom. We should all be careful to avail ourselves of the benefits they have to offer both the present generation and the one that will follow us."

— attributed to William Wilberforce

Am I teaching enough?

Dear mamas, I know you're fretting about "not teaching enough." I know you're concerned that you aren't doing it right. The end of the "school year" may be approaching, and you're worried that your kids aren't going to measure up.

Take a deep breath, and remember why you homeschool. You have chosen an alternative path. So no, you won't measure up to the government school system.

But you don't want to, really, do you?

You are free from the mandates that state and federal government impose on every public school system in America. You're free to spend more time on a difficult math problem. You're free to discuss that good book you just read with the kids. You're free to have a long conversation about capitalism vs. socialism. You're free to allow your special needs child more time to learn to write.

Just because the government schools look official, with their scope and sequence and their coded names for programs, it doesn't mean their methods are producing incredible results. If they were, you probably wouldn't be homeschooling, would you?

Don't fear what you didn't want. Let them have their methods. Be bold with your alternative. Take confidence in the fact that God gave these children to YOU. Don't fret. The very fact that you're concerned and anxious for their education assures me that they will succeed. It will look different from public school, and that is precisely the point.

5 things about homeschooling that government can't comprehend:

1. It doesn't take 12 years to educate a child.
2. A homeschooling parent doesn't need a college degree to teach their own children.
3. "Grade level" is a recent invention.
4. Socialization happens everywhere, not in a classroom.
5. Homeschooling can be free or very inexpensive.

Even if you're a new homeschooler, you are paving the way for someone to come after you, whether it's a neighbor, a church friend, or even your own children.

Embrace not being like everyone else. You'll be ready to pass that encouragement on to someone else very soon!

A long range weapon

Our culture hates children. It wants to kill them, and if it cannot kill them, it wants mutilate them and weaponize them.

But the Bible says, *"Behold, children are a heritage from the LORD, the fruit of the womb a reward. Like arrows in the hand of a warrior are the children of one's youth. Blessed is the man who fills his quiver with them!"* (Psalm 127:3-5)

They are a blessing, and they are arrows!

"Giving your children an anti-Christian education is not an expectation that Scripture puts on parents. When Psalm 127 speaks of children as arrows in the hand of a mighty warrior, it has in mind releasing those arrows when they are prepared.

Ancient warriors usually fashioned their own arrows. They would work long hours, making sure their arrows were balanced and shaped just so, to be able to fly straight and true. They understood that the future of their entire nation depended on these arrows. They did not dare release them until they were completely ready.

We should follow their example."
(Israel Wayne, Education: Does God Have an Opinion?)[viii]

Friends, are we sharpening arrows?

Interruptions

"A man's heart plans his way, but the LORD directs his steps." (Proverbs 16:11 NKJV)

In a perfect world, there are all sorts of things you'd like to get done. But we don't live in a perfect world, do we?

Interruptions are a normal and expected part of the homeschooling process. But that doesn't mean you have to be discouraged by the interruptions or that they have to derail your entire day (or week or year!). The question is, how do we best handle these interruptions when they do come?

1. Put away electronic devices—sometimes it helps to physically remove them from the room you are in so that they are not a temptation, either for you or for your kids.

2. Be careful not to become a slave to your schedule, and be ready to change it up if it isn't working for you. You can have structure while also having flexibility.

3. It's important to remember that not every interruption has to make you stop working on your original task. Make a note and move on. While there are plenty of situations that will demand you attention right away, if a request doesn't need to be done immediately, or if you're working on a more pressing task, write down the need on a notepad. Writing down non-urgent requests, or other tasks that pop into your head, instead of tackling them right away, and drawing your attention away from what you're doing, is a good way to cut down on interruptions and keep track of everything that you need to get to.

4. With small children: train them, when appropriate, to wait.

5. With older children: give them a timeframe: "I'll be finished with what I'm doing in 20 minutes."

6. Schedule buffer time in your day. Allow for more time to do a project or lesson than you think you'll need.

7. Count it all joy! Having a negative response will only exacerbate the situation. It's better

to meet the interruptions with a smile and simply take care of what needs to be taken care of. Then move on with the rest of your day.

Whether your homeschool day has been upended, or just parenting in general:

- Remember that you are setting an example for your kids
- Ask yourself: what can be salvaged? Can the kids continue learning on their own, or do you need to stop everything to handle an emergency?
- Would a snack, coffee, walk outside, or another break help reset?
- Deal with it mentally - face it, handle it, move on
- Evaluate expectations - and expect the unexpected
- Remember this motto: *People over things; people over plans.*

Finally, realize that failed plans are not only an expected part of life but also precious opportunities to learn to trust the Lord. Conversations happen that wouldn't have happened, precious teaching moments pop up, spiritual disciplines are honed (like patience and endurance), we are forced to trust the Lord more, and we end up in places we never would have gone.

Light a fire

Education should light a fire in kids, not just check off a list. If they encounter a niche topic they love, they should be given time to obsess about it and become an expert. This is what teaches children to love learning.

If your son is obsessed with ninjas, dive deep into the history of ninjas. If he is obsessed with WWII, dive deep into the history of WWII. Don't rush through, trying to check boxes and complete a transcript.

Throw fuel on the fire.

Let something else take a backseat.

Encourage research.

Encourage rabbit trails.

Lead the way!

Expose them to as much as you can, but don't force them to be professional students.

Experts vs. moms

American teachers spend their summers brushing up on professional development. But they're not brushing up on ways to inspire learning, improve reading, or advance academics. No, they're increasingly forced to learn about special treatment of gay and trans kids, combating white privilege, the evils of colonialism, repackaging DEI and SEL, and what to do in an emergency (like school shootings).

And the public education system has created a bureaucratic nightmare of terms and practices that you literally do need a teaching degree to understand, because they keep making stuff up.

Meanwhile, test scores have fallen so much that the goal posts have been moved. Expectations are lowered, and kids are passed through the system with fake grades so that the district gets their funding.

They've left the simple methods of education behind and have done what government always does: made it more complicated, time-consuming, and expensive.

Dear homeschool mom: it's not complicated. The methods are easy, and the curriculum choices are abundant. Anyone can homeschool, just like everyone used to, before big government got involved.

So, when you feel tempted to compare your kids to what you think the public school is doing, remember: education is not what it used to be. Your kids are so much better off at home.

The made-up science of "levels"

Public school keeps kids in boxes by making them read "at their level."

Let me let you in on a little secret: kids don't have "levels." They are unique individuals who learn at different speeds.

That means that some kids need to spend several years in easy readers to gain confidence and enjoy reading, while other kids will read full-length classic novels before they are ten years old.

Both are okay.

Instead of pigeonholing kids, keeping them back, or making them feel inadequate, let kids read what they can read, and ignore those lists with made-up "levels."

Do babies crawl on schedule?

Children do not sit up, crawl, or walk on a schedule created by bureaucrats. Neither should they be expected to read, write, or learn math basics on a schedule created by bureaucrats.

So, mamas (and daddies), don't fret. Don't stress yourself or your child over "benchmarks" or "should be." Every child is unique. You could very well have advanced readers and slow readers in your family. The same goes for math, writing, comprehension, logic, and more.

The goal is to give your children a love of learning. When they have that, they will pick up the mechanics. Be patient and encouraging. Sometimes slow and steady truly does win the race.

From my experience, all of the elementary disciplines can be learned by the age of ten. Some kids will master them much earlier, and some will need every bit of that time. Don't panic. Don't give up! Just keep moving forward.

Creative ways to accomplish your tasks

While your children are young, it's hard to find times for those routines and rituals that you want (and need).

Even if you get up early to read and pray, a fussy baby or an early-rising toddler often wakes up ready for the day. Reading a good book without interruption seems nearly impossible. Daily devotions with babies get derailed more often than not. Home-cooked hot meals are often sacrificed for sandwiches. Exercise feels impossible for more than five minutes. And don't even bring up the piles of laundry waiting to be washed or folded!

You will definitely have to adjust your expectations, but you really can find efficient ways to include the important things in your day!

Over the years, I found a few ways to adjust. First of all, praying can happen at any time. Bible reading can also be Bible listening, with an audio Bible and one earbud in your ear. Trade your private Bible reading for family Bible reading (babies and toddlers in tow!). If even family devotions get sidelined, switch to scripture memory songs for everyone to listen to and sing.

Whether you use a slow cooker or pressure cooker, work smarter, not harder! Double the ingredients, and put a second meal in the freezer, or use the leftovers for lunches. Double a batch of beans, rice, pasta, potatoes, or taco meat.

There are many ways to get physical activity, even with lots of children. Walk around the backyard while the children play. Play at the park *with* the kids. Put baby on your back or in a stroller and walk while the kids ride bikes. Show the children how to do jumping jacks, sit ups, play catch, and work in the flower beds or garden.

The laundry? Teach the children to sort, wash, fold, and put away! We used to do this as a team with some music playing or an old favorite movie on in the background. And by the time my kids were all about 8-10 years old, they were doing their own laundry.

Think outside the box, and you'll find creative ways to accomplish the most important things.

Burnout

Have you ever experienced "homeschool burnout?" It often happens several months into a school year. Maybe it's winter. Maybe you feel like a robot. Maybe you're wondering why you ever decided to homeschool. You're thinking you need a way out.

Now is the time to be pro-active. How can you stave off these negative feelings?

Remember: you are a family, not a school. Live that way. Who's in charge here? You are! Change things up if you need to!

Is the stress of "falling behind" fueling your burnout? Don't get hung up on "standards." Public schools have standards, and they lower them regularly. How's that working out? Instead, focus on consistent progress.

Think outside the "school year." Just because everyone else is hitting the books hard, you don't have to. Re-think your schedule. Do a big project together. Spend time with a great book. Do a special unit study. Refresh your home. Go out of town.

Rethink your approach to education. If a book or curriculum (or even a subject) isn't working in your house, it's okay to let it go. Maybe for a season, or maybe forever. You are the parent, and you are in charge. Be bold and confident!

Don't compare your home/school/family to anyone else's. Theodore Rooservelt said, "Comparison is the thief of joy." It only makes you stressed. Instead, ask God for wisdom. Seek His will for your family.

Finally, if all of your homeschooling methods are working well, don't throw them out based on a whim! The winter/mid-year slump is normal. Just take a break and resume lessons when you're ready.

Surrender all

Are you familiar with the old hymn, "I Surrender All?" When you sing those words, they can be convicting. Do we truly surrender all to Jesus?

Dear parents, this also includes your homeschool. Some days we feel nervous, anxious, incapable, or just plain tired. We may worry that our sons won't get into college, or that our daughters won't be ready to manage a home. We might wonder if they will graduate at all. And we pray that they will walk in righteousness all the days of their lives.

It is not we who accomplish these things in our children. It is the Lord. We are called to raise them up in the nurture and admonition of the Lord (Ephesians 6:4). We are the sowers; we plant the seed and wait for the harvest. But we do not always get to be the harvesters. Sometimes we must wait. *Wait on the LORD: be of good courage, and he shall strengthen your heart: wait, I say, on the LORD.* (Psalm 27:14 NKJV)

All to Jesus I surrender,
All to Him I freely give.
I will ever love and trust Him,
In His presence daily live.

I surrender all.
I surrender all.
All to thee my blessed Savior
I surrender all.

Let's talk about curriculum

Curriculum. Homeschool parents everywhere vary widely; they either love it, or agonize over it, or even hate it. So, let's talk about how to use it!

If you buy a curriculum for your little boy or girl, and the concepts seem too hard, don't just assume the curriculum is bad. It might be that your child is not ready. Put it on the shelf for a few months and try again.

If you were loving a curriculum (or a subject) and life interrupted it, don't just start all over with something new. Do a quick review and pick up where you left off! In doing this, you'll be less likely to miss important concepts or interesting stories.

If you don't finish a curriculum by an arbitrary calendar date, don't just ditch school and start a new level next at a new arbitrary calendar date. Ignore the date and continue the learning! Again, think about concepts that are important for your students to understand.

Break outside of the government school mindset. You are a family. You are not a school. Let curriculum be your tool, not your master.

And yeah, it's also okay to discover that a curriculum just isn't working for your family. Sell it to another homeschool family and move on. This is the beauty of private home education: *you* are in charge!

Enjoy the journey

It's going to be okay. You taught your baby how to eat from a spoon. You taught your toddler to walk and run. You taught your children to talk, count, sing songs, brush their teeth, and use the potty.

Your ability to teach your children doesn't end when they turn 5.

You may have decided to homeschool, but now you're in a panic. Can I do this? Will I mess up my kids? Will they be behind? Will they go to college?

It's going to be okay.

Take it one day, one prayer at a time. Enjoy the journey. You're raising a family; you're not running a school.

Off the beaten path is the best place to be

There is very little room for individuality in public education. Everyone's education is standardized.

Oh, how boring!

We were meant to grow in our strengths! Home education allows room for the basic academic schedule *and* room for interests to grow, time for hobbies, and room for chasing tangents.

Within each family, there is a wide range of personalities, interests, strengths, and weaknesses. Each of your children will be very different. You can see this by how they dress, work, play, laugh, and mature.

Can you imagine trying to harness them all into one "standard child" mold?

Standards are a guide. Feel free to go off the beaten path.

Scriptures for mothers to pray

"May our sons in their youth be like plants full grown, our daughters like corner pillars cut for the structure of a palace;" (Psalm 144:12)

"Let me hear in the morning of your steadfast love, for in you I trust. Make me know the way I should go, for to you I lift up my soul." (Psalm 143:8)

"The Lord is near to the brokenhearted and saves the crushed in spirit."(Psalm 34:18)

"When the righteous cry for help, the Lord hears and delivers them out of all their troubles." (Psalm 34:17)

"Out of the depths I cry to you, O Lord! O Lord, hear my voice! Let your ears be attentive to the voice of my pleas for mercy! If you, O Lord, should mark iniquities, O Lord, who could stand? But with you there is forgiveness, that you may be feared. I wait for the Lord, my soul waits, and in his word I hope; my soul waits for the Lord more

than watchmen for the morning, more than watchmen for the morning. O Israel, hope in the Lord! For with the Lord there is steadfast love, and with him is plentiful redemption. And he will redeem Israel from all his iniquities."
(Psalm 130:1-8)

You can (and should) learn with your children

"I'm terrible at math."

"I hate science."

"I don't remember any history."

That's okay. The first step is admitting you have a problem. Really!

You are not the first homeschool parent to re-learn the things they taught you in school. The surprising thing is, you may learn to love, or at least appreciate these subjects.

I can't count how many moms have told me that they sat with their children and learned alongside them. They suddenly loved history because they had never read it like this before! They didn't know Bible study could be so deep! They were never taught that God created the world and that the Old Testament is a history book!

Don't let your own school experience hold you back from enjoying the world of learning with your kids. Don't let your fears convince you that you can't teach what you hated in school.

You've been given a second chance. Go all in!

The ministry of motherhood

You think, "If I had a ministry or a meaningful career, I'd be making a real difference."

Mothers have been given the greatest privilege: to nurture and shape tiny humans, and by that, to shape the future.

It is such a big thing, but honestly, it can be a hard thing. It's hard to keep the big picture in mind when your son is talking back or your toddler won't sleep. You get caught up in the immediate stress or frustration of the moment. You might lose your patience, get angry, or wallow in self-pity.

Dear mom, please don't underestimate your value right here, right now. Don't trade this enormous trust for worldly gain or even great feelings of accomplishment. There is no corporation that needs you as much as your family does. There is no ministry more important than the one in your home.

It's been said that motherhood is a marathon, not a sprint. It *is* a long commitment. And let me tell you, no matter how enticing those things outside your home can be, you'll be constantly pulled in multiple directions emotionally, mentally, and physically if you give into them.

Jesus said, *"My yoke is easy, and my burden is light."* (Matthew 11:30) Don't desire a heavier yoke. Accept the enormous gift of motherhood for what it is. Pour your heart into *this* ministry. Build God's kingdom instead of a corporate empire.

I understand perfectly that many times both parents must work to make ends meet. This is not intended to bring guilt on you. I've been there, too. But I also know the feeling of thinking there's something more "out there." Trust me, there's no job more important than motherhood.

Homeschooling isn't a magic wand

Homeschooling doesn't insulate your child from the world. It won't make your kids nicer, more responsible, or smarter. It won't make them better Christians, or Christians at all.

But what homeschooling gives you is *time* to parent. With your children under your influence (instead of the state and their peers), time is a blessing.

Time for manners.

Time for responsibility training.

Time to talk.

Time for deep Bible study.

Time for quality academics.

Time with you.

You have been given a very short window of time to raise your sons and daughters to adulthood. But that window of time can be stretched when they are home with you.

"Hear, O Israel: The Lord our God, the Lord is one. Love the Lord your God with all your heart and with all your soul and with all your strength. These commandments that I give you today are to be on your hearts. Impress them on your children. Talk about them when you sit at home and when you walk along the road, when you lie down and when you get up. Tie them as symbols on your hands and bind them on your foreheads. Write them on the doorframes of your houses and on your gates." (Deuteronomy 6:4-9)

Make the most of childhood by being there. Be the primary influence on your children. Talk to them, disciple them, and be a shield between them and the world.

Homeschooling is more about HOME than school.

The lurking danger in the safest small towns

I love small towns. It's where you'll find friendly people, delicious diners, and a slower pace. Everyone knows everyone. Everyone looks out for each other. Kids grow up in a bit of a protected bubble from the "big city" atmosphere.

Or they used to.

Now the big city culture comes right into your homes, thanks to the internet. Children surrounded by close family and caring neighbors are still being exposed to the most extreme facets of the culture when they are given a tablet, a smartphone, or plopped in front of a smart tv. And have you noticed? They're *all* smart TVs now.

Moms and dads, I've said it before, and I'll keep saying it: there's nothing useful or educational on the internet that your kids can't live without. They won't be smarter just because they play educational games online. They won't get a better tech job someday because they have a tablet today.

But they will have access to a thousand new ideas that you haven't considered. This is no exaggeration.

Wherever you live, the number one thing you can do to preserve the innocence and hearts of your children is to shut off the internet and let them be kids.

They will survive. And you won't regret it.

Public school won't fix disobedience

Guess what? You're not the only homeschool parent with a disobedient child!

Do you know something else? Homeschooling isn't causing disobedience.

Way too often, I read about parents who have a defiant son or daughter, and their first instinct is to send the child off to public school.

Wait!!

Public school won't cure disobedience. It only prolongs a deeper issue. A disobedient child is a sinful child. It is explicitly the duty of parents to shepherd their child's hearts and train them up in the way they should go.

It's not easy, I know. Parenting is not easy. (How many times have my husband and I said this to each other in exasperation??)

If your child rebels during math, put the math aside for a bit and deal with the rebellion. Math can wait. School can wait. Dealing with disobedience cannot wait.

Mothers and fathers, child training is your most important job. And that means training in obedience and respect. Sending kids to public school will not accomplish that. It only shifts the problem, allowing it to fester and grow. Do your child a huge favor and deal with the problem now.

A few tips:

1. Pray for discernment
2. Set family rules if you haven't already
3. Calmly remind children each morning of rules and consequences
4. Drink your coffee (I'm only sort of kidding)
5. Consider a learning issue or a curriculum issue
6. Rinse and repeat (it won't change overnight)

God gave you these children, and He already gave you what you need to raise them.

Be the church

We are a society that is quick to view government programs as the norm. Too often, Christians do this, too. Government is a mess. It should be a last, desperate measure when someone needs help.

Including government schools.

Be the person who helps others find a way out of public school. There are many ways to do this:

1. **Be a present helper**: offer free child care once a week, give the children rides to co-op, be the surrogate parent at co-op or field trips, or feed the family every Tuesday evening. Sometimes you want to help but you can't do it all; consider teaming up with another family or two to meet these needs and spread the responsibility around.

2. **Contribute financially**. If you have the funds to bless another family, consider these options: purchasing curriculum, buying or delivering groceries, giving a gift of a monthly sum,

paying for tutors or co-op fees, or even hiring a parent to work remotely for your business.

3. **Tutor in your own home.** Do you have a desire to teach or help? Offer free tutoring! This might involve helping with math lessons once a week or overseeing an entire curriculum for a parent who desperately needs assistance.

4. **Start a cooperative.** Outside help is usually a tremendous blessing for parents who must work or who might have other special circumstances. If you like the idea of starting a cooperative, consider the needs of parents in special situations and assemble a leadership team who will keep this in mind. Look for ways to make it work for as many families as possible.

5. **Offer a facility.** Pastors, business owners, and others who have a meeting facility are a treasure! If you are in one of these positions, and are looking for ways to support the homeschool community, consider the ministry that your building could be in this way.

Build homeschool community wherever you are, whether it's with 5 people or 50. It's not about forming clubs and groups; it's about freeing children and parents from the public school system for good.

Will I mess up my kids?

This is a common worry, especially among new homeschooling moms. Since most of us are not "trained professionals," we assume we're never going to educate quite properly.

It's hard to get worldly ideas out of our heads, like grade-level checklists, test scores, scope and sequence, and other bureaucratic mumbo-jumbo. But while the government schools look very polished and official from the outside, what's happening on the inside is less than stellar.

Academics are increasingly traded for activism. Students are being sexualized at younger and younger ages. And the curriculum is entirely taught from a secular humanist worldview.

No, you can't possibly mess your kids up by keeping them out of that.

Remember, *the wisdom of this world is foolishness with God.* (1 Corinthians 3:19 KJV) Next time you worry about messing up your kids, ask yourself where that idea came from?

Making memories

Little family traditions that may seem insignificant right now are building powerful memories for your children.

Maybe you make French toast every Friday morning, or read aloud in the backyard when the weather is nice. Maybe you don't have these little traditions yet.

Trust me, they have an impact!

Giving your kids special family rituals builds a family culture in the home, and gives them fond days to remember when they're grown and away from home.

I have read some great ideas over the years, such as only serving chocolate milk Saturday mornings, or letting the kids pile up in mom's bed to watch a favorite family show before breakfast. We look forward to a pumpkin-scented candle every September 1, and making snow ice cream if we get snow in Texas!

So, what can you do that's simple and special?

A special breakfast recipe once a week? Regular movie night? Collecting and pressing the first yellow leaves each autumn? A favorite song playlist for housecleaning day?

Think of the little things you remember from your childhood, or from visiting your grandparents. Take note of what your children ask for repeatedly, and make it "our thing." I guarantee you, these are the moments they will remember.

There's so much more to life than school

Sometimes we have entire months go by without doing any school work. I used to try to find "educational activities" to keep my kids busy when life got crazy, because it made me feel like we were doing something important.

But as the years went by, I realized that real life is just as educational as the school books. We had a time recently where the months stretched on with very little school work.

My grandfather was in his last days on this earth, and I took turns with my mom, sitting with him and holding his hand as we watched westerns on TV or butterflies outside his window. Planning his funeral and managing his estate took up many days after he passed.

A friend of my children died, and we spent many days processing, talking, and joining others for counseling.

Thanksgiving, winter illness, Christmas, and moving to a new home all combined to make for a very busy season.

There were days when my kids did their basics (math, grammar, and reading) and many, many days where we didn't even do that. But this was definitely not my first rodeo. We'd had life take priority over school before, and we learned that school is not the most important thing.

Don't get me wrong, it's important. I'm all for an excellent education. But I'm also interested in my kids living real life, including the hard parts. They have had the luxury (if you call it that) of mourning in the safety and comfort of home, sleeping in when sick, going ice skating with friends on a Monday morning, helping with the move, and more. They aren't at school all day while life passes them by.

It does not take 12 years of 8-hour days to educate children. And there's so much more to life than school.

It's okay if you don't have an "Instagram" homeschool

Would you like to see how a day in our life looks?

Each morning, my dear children wake up with a smile on their face and a song in their heart. They joyfully gather at the breakfast table for the nutritious oatmeal I have prepared, and listen as I read the Bible aloud for an hour.

They move on to happily doing housework, and then beg to begin their academic lessons. Every moment of the day is pure delight as they seek to become more intelligent, more mature, and more spiritual.

When Dad comes home, they welcome him with questions, conversation, and admonitions to relax in his favorite chair. The evening is spent in important debates about politics and theology. We finally drop into bed, exhausted but exhilarated by such a fulfilling day, and I go to sleep thankful for the easiest job in the world.

Ha.

That's more like an Instagram post than anyone's reality! I wish it were true. It is my goal. But alas! My children and I are sadly human. We each have a sin nature that pulls us to be selfish, lazy, and prideful. I am reminded of this hour-by-hour, day-by-day.

If your homeschool is not the picture-perfect fantasy you had at the beginning, just know that you are not alone. Our job as mothers is a hard one and a necessary one. It is also the most important job there is. It is rarely easy. (Sometimes it is!)

Don't throw in the towel when it's a struggle. Take your struggle to God. Ask for His forgiveness, His grace, and His help. (Hebrews 4:16)

And then, as Elisabeth Elliot always said, "do the next thing."

A personalized education

Don't ever let anyone tell you that you're homeschooling the wrong way. Education is discipleship. Homeschooling is parenting with school books. There are as many ways to educate your child as there are to dress him.

The most important thing to remember is that you are the parents God entrusted with your children, and no one else. You need to do what's best for your family, your children.

If you do read classic novels, or don't, it's okay.

If your kids learn to read at 3 or at 8, it's okay.

If you use textbooks for everything and never do crafts, it's okay.

If your kids graduate with full college scholarships or go to work on the farm, it's okay.

Public schools are factories and children are the product. The product must meet certain requirements and must be as standard as possible.

Thank goodness your child is not standard! They are a unique individual created in the image of God. You know all children are different if you have two or more of them. Your family is not standard, either. Embrace that!

Do what works. Choose your methods and curriculum with prayer and wisdom, and not from peer pressure or social media pressure. Seek help when you need it, or ask for advice from a trusted source. But don't ever let anyone tell you that you're homeschooling the wrong way.

Be a family, not a school.

Dear Ladies

If you believe that your husband isn't smart enough, Christian enough, or whatever-enough to lead your family, you have bought the lie of feminism.

If you think you have to lead because he doesn't agree with you, you have bought the lie of feminism.

If you blame your bad attitude, rebellion, or terrible decisions on your husband, you have bought the lie of feminism.

Feminism is poison. It cripples families because it perverts the natural, God-designed order of the home. Men were created by God to lead. If your husband isn't leading (or even if you think he isn't leading), consider that you might have made him too miserable to try.

Christian women hold a mighty power: making a home. It can be mundane household chores, or it can be giving life and purpose to all who live there.

You decide. Get out of the way. Do your part, not your husband's part.

Don't be like Eve, who asked, "Did God really say...?"

The pursuit of Christ

Do your children have their "thing?"

Musical talent, movie buff, athletics, classic literature, horses, art, WWII, cooking, or computers are just a handful of interests that our kids could zero in on. It's fun to watch each of our children dig deeper into an interest or special gift, and homeschooling makes it possible to let them pursue their passions.

Encourage them to read just a little more, practice a little longer, and get a little better. This is not only fun and educational; it is character building!

But, more than anything, encourage your children to pursue Christ. Encourage them to read the Bible the most, to know God more, and to be the most passionate about Him. God made us unique and gave us our talents and interests, and all of this is for His glory.

As the Westminster Catechism states, "The chief end of man is to glorify God and enjoy Him forever."

Point your children daily to their Creator.

Resist the urge to run a school

Did you know that all of your children do not have to have the same education? They may not take all of the same courses, complete grade levels at the same time, read all the same books, or graduate at the same age.

They are unique and individual. God created them this way.

Remember the *home* part of homeschool. Allow each of your children to be who God made them to be while you educate them with the basics.

Manage your home. Don't create a school.

Be a family, not a classroom.

As the years go by, your circumstances may change, your needs may change, and your budget may change. Your children will grow and mature, developing interests that are uniquely their own.

There is nothing standard about your children, so don't try to standardize their education. Teach them to read, write, and compute, and then let them branch out from there!

Creating your own game plan

Imagine the possibilities when you don't have the public school counselor telling you *what* your kids should learn and when.

Imagine putting an emphasis on scripture, worldview, and logic!

Imagine building a family business together!

Imagine passing down your knowledge and abilities to your children!

Are you handy with wood? Do you play an instrument? Are you proficient in three languages? Do you raise animals or food? Do you sew, cook, or build things?

You have a built-in custom curriculum for your children in the things you do well. Use that!

In days gone by, families passed down their skills and personal knowledge to the next generation, and the next generation, and so on.

You can do that in your homeschool as well.

Behind, behind, behind

Have you worried that your homeschool children are "behind?" Has someone told you that they are, or scared you with that possibility? The answer is probably an emphatic "yes!"

I guess if the public school scope and sequence is still a measuring stick, you might be concerned about "3rd grade math" or "8th grade English." But if you're not at public school, don't be concerned.

I'll be blunt: even the public schools are failing to keep kids from being "behind." It's their system, and they can't even make it work. Just ask all the teachers who are forced to pass kids on to the next grade whether they know the material or not.

So, take a deep breath and let them have their failing system. You get a new one. You get freedom, individuality, and life.

Don't look back.

Teach your children to write well

Good communicators have the ability to change the world if they want to, and that's a really big deal. And that's why you should teach your children to write well. Writing well can also create people who speak well.

Christian parents, just as Esther was put in a certain place at a certain time to do a very important work, our children were also "born for such a time as this." The culture we live in is disturbing, to say the least. Some days it causes me to mourn that my children and grandchildren must grow up in this ugly world. But then I remember that God knew exactly what He was doing when He gave us kids for the 21st century.

So, let's equip them for important work. Let's give them the tools they need to communicate God's love and biblical principles to a confused and hurting world. Yes, they need some high school credits, and a great writing course will definitely fill that need, but let's look beyond credits and educate Christian soldiers to lead future generations.

There is no such thing as behind

Children are individuals. They have different personalities, different interests, different talents, and different needs. Some walk and talk early. Some walk and talk later. Some are ready to read at three years old. Some don't learn until age 9. Some can name all the states at 5. Some can name all the dinosaurs. Some just want to play in the dirt.

Children are individuals. They are not advanced or behind. They are not first grade or fifth grade. They are unique.

Let them be who they are.

Watch for clues about what they're ready for. If you think they're ready to read, try it. Go slow and easy, with very short lessons. You'll know within a few weeks if they're ready or not. Do the same with handwriting and math. And don't be alarmed if each of these three things progresses at a different pace. They may be ready for one but not the others.

Children come into this world as individuals. (Experienced moms know that those personalities show up very early.) They will mature and grow and learn at different paces. And that's very normal.

Sing to them. Read to them. Talk to them. Play with them. And as you feel led, introduce learning activities to them. Don't worry about their age or supposed grade level. Pray for discernment, and gently guide them. And if they don't match up to the world's timeline, that's ok.

Be a family, not a school.

Managing your home

How do you find balance with homeschooling and everything else? The answer: a little bit of planning and some clever multitasking.

To-do lists keep me focused. I have three whiteboards around the house for this, for myself and the kids.

Double-up on food prep. I like to whip up a batch of muffins or sausage burritos while I'm preparing supper, or start a casserole for dinner first thing in the morning.

Set a timer. You can accomplish a lot in 15 minutes. Set a timer and fold a load of laundry or load the dishwasher while the kids do a workbook or read.

Give the kids more responsibility. Teach them one new household chore, and take one (or three!) off your plate.

Teach the kids to make meals (simple or elaborate, depending on their age). In time, they will be able to make a sandwich, cook eggs and toast, and eventually a full supper for the family.

Let go of the world's standards

When doubts about your homeschooling start to creep in, examine the source.

When you think your kids are behind, ask yourself who gave you the idea of behind? It is probably the K-12 system that permeates our society. Don't let this made-up standard guilt you into grade-level fear. If your child is progressing in their education, you are on the right track.

When you think your kids aren't involved in enough activities, ask yourself who decides *what is enough*? Is it the social norm of having every free minute of a child's life scheduled? If your child has time to get bored, you are on the right track.

When you think your high schooler needs to spend their teen years pleasing some future college admissions officer, ask yourself if this time is spent wisely? Is it the pressure from the world to have a fancy degree? If your child is preparing to be a critical thinker, a smart money manager, and has a biblical worldview, you are on the right path.

When you think you're not teaching enough, once again, ask who defines "enough?"

In most cases, these doubts stem from the standard American public education mindset. Even when the origin of these ideas is fuzzy, we let them cause us so much anxiety and fear. These are worldly standards. They are not God's standards.

You really have to begin homeschooling by de-schooling your brain. Throw out the public school model. Throw out the "extracurricular" frenzy. Throw out the grade-level standards.

Raise children who will be individuals, just as God created them. Raise thinkers, creators, and world-changers.

Shelter is not a bad word

Dear moms, while the world is pushing an increasingly evil narrative everywhere we turn, we don't have to feel overpowered or defeated. The incessant messages try to tell our kids that transsexuals are cool, that atheism is truth, that fear is normal, that males are tyrannical, that communism is good, that pedophilia is love, and that God is dead.

We are in a desperate battle for our children's hearts and minds. The situation is dire. It feels like too much.

Hold the line.

Moms, you are the walls of the castle. You are the protective wing of the hen. You are the she-bear.

You are so much to your children. They need you to shield them from the evil while training them in the good. They need you to show them a fearless faith in God. They need to see that the joy of the Lord is your strength.

There is nothing new under the sun. God has seen all this before. He is not shocked or scared. Neither should you be. You and your children were created for such a time as this.

If you are feeling the weight of this sinful world, draw closer to Christ. Read just a little bit more scripture each day. Spend a bit of extra time in prayer. Sing one more hymn. And teach all of this to your children.

Shelter is good. Use it fiercely.

What qualifies someone to teach a child?

Is it the two years of "basics" every college student takes?

Is it the multiple classes on classroom management and parent communication that is part of a teaching certification?

Is it being forced to teach to a standardized test?

Is it passing kids through each grade level no matter what they have or haven't learned?

Is it being forced to use gender pronouns on kids at school while keeping it from the parents?

Is it all the equity training teachers must attend throughout the school year?

Or could it possibly be a parent who loves their child more than anyone else could? Could it possibly be the authority given by God to teach, train, and disciple their children with wisdom and knowledge, and to raise them up in the admonition of the Lord?

Maybe we can let go of the golden calf of "qualification" and embrace a biblical worldview again. The world's standards are so far below God's standards for knowledge and wisdom, and especially who should be discipling children. Worrying about qualification is living in fear of man.

You are qualified to teach your children.

What does homeschooling look like?

It looks like gathering at the kitchen table to begin workbooks at 8:00, lunch at noon, and finishing by 3.

And it looks like read-aloud time at 10, math sprawled on the bed, a science lesson on video after lunch, and a history lesson that lasts for two hours.

And it looks like getting the hard subjects done while the toddler naps, passing out snacks to keep math fun, and running around in the backyard for exercise.

And it looks like 1 hour of a bit of handwriting, a bit of reading, a page of math problems, and a YouTube video.

And it looks like 2 straight days of homework, writing assignments, science experiments, reading historical documents, and algebra 2, while working a part-time job the rest of the week.

And it looks like mom teaching lessons in the afternoon when she gets home from her part-time job, dad helping with math at night, and science lessons at a homeschool co-op on Wednesdays.

Homeschooling looks like a hundred different things in a hundred different families. It's learning at home, on your schedule, with your favorite materials, on every budget.

It looks like HOME.

-*Anyone Can Homeschool* by Nicki Truesdell[ix]

Keep your own schedule

Winter blues. Summer heat. Cabin fever. Blahs. Homeschool burnout.

It's real.

Many moms right now are thinking they just want a break, but they'll get behind. The kids are going crazy.

TAKE. THAT. BREAK. Sleep in. Have a lazy day, or a lazy week. Do something fun you've been putting off. Or just catch up on rest. Pop some corn and watch movies in pajamas.

There is no such thing as "behind" in homeschooling. You are a family. You are not a school. Stress is from the world. Shut the world out and nurture your family.

"Come unto me, all ye that labor and are heavy laden, and I will give you rest. Take my yoke upon you, and learn of me; for I am meek and lowly in heart: and ye shall find rest unto your souls. For

my yoke is easy, and my burden is light." (Matthew 11:28-30 KJV)

Cramming or discipling?

Homeschool parents with teenagers often fall into the trap of cramming. Cramming their child's school days with every possible opportunity, cramming their transcript with all the extras, and cramming their years with impressive credits.

We buy into the fear that if we don't stuff their transcript with hundreds of things that look great on paper, we are ruining their lives. And while we're busy trying to make colleges love our kids, we often neglect the most important things!

Bible study doesn't matter much to a college admissions program. You can't prove a biblical worldview on an entrance exam. And forget about choosing a godly spouse, raising children, managing money, or voting wisely. These can't be measured, and they are infinitely more important than GPAs and scholarships.

Don't fall into the trap.

Whatever form your homeschooling takes, whatever future plans your child has, don't cram them so full of worldly achievements that you neglect their hearts and souls.

The teen years are often their last years at home. Make them count. Now is the time to talk, discuss, counsel, and exhort. And you can't do much of these important things when their to-do list is a mile long.

Give that to-do list a second perusal. What items are just there because the world says they should be? What is truly important? Whose wisdom are you following?

Strength and dignity

Some days are so great that you smile at night and think, "I've got this figured out." And then the next day is a mess, and you think you're a failure.

But you're not failing. It's not your fault. It's not the kids' fault. It's real life. Babies are happy, and babies are fussy. Laundry gets caught up, and laundry gets dreadfully behind. Kids obey cheerfully, and kids disobey shockingly. We have smooth days, and we have tough days. Or weeks. Or months.

This is life!

Circumstances aren't our whole life. They are mostly little things that come and go. Sometimes they are bigger, and harder, and last longer than we think we can handle. But the Christian woman has no reason to be tossed to and fro emotionally. *Strength and dignity are her clothing, and she laughs at the time to come.* (Proverbs 31:25)

Moms, we are given a great responsibility: to manage homes and to raise a new generation. It is no small calling. It is also no small task. Some days are indeed difficult, but they are not impossible.

Remember the Proverbs 31 woman? Whatever she was given to do, she did with dignity, confidence, and assurance. She laughed! Her struggles are not mentioned, but she had them.

Whatever you're doing at home is better

It only takes a few minutes of scrolling social media to be reminded about what's happening in public schools.

Principals throwing a high school boys' drag show in the gym.

A school taking elementary kids on a field trip to a gay bar.

Another school assigning 3rd graders a paper on eating babies.

A high school boy being crowned homecoming queen.

A school scrambling to remove actual porn from the library.

A teacher commenting in a group about her school's transgender training (for staff and students) that she's not allowed to tell parents about.

And yet, every day, homeschool moms beat themselves up about not measuring up. They're afraid they will ruin their kids. They think their curriculum isn't rigorous enough, or that they will get behind.

Mamas, keep on giving your kids a childhood. Keep up the story time. Keep singing with them. Keep encouraging their strengths and being patient with their weaknesses.

Because whatever you're doing in your homeschool is a thousand times more valuable than the twisted assignments that are taking the place of real academics in the buildings they call school.

"What grade is this book for?"

I can't answer that question. Each child is unique. We need to stop putting kids in grade-level boxes, and instead, let them grow at their own pace.

If a book looks good, and your child can't read it yet, read it to him. If a book is an easy reader and your advanced child wants to read it for fun, let him!

Some six-year-olds can read books that some ten-year-olds can't. Some ten-year-olds can do math on a level that some high schoolers can't. That's why "grade level" is so unhelpful. It's not an accurate representation of intelligence or ability. It just represents a public education list of boxes to check.

Moms and dads, don't get antsy if your child is not "on grade-level." Continuous progress is the goal. And that looks different for every child, of every age, at every house. Just as kids have their physical growth spurts at different ages, they will speed up and slow down in academics. It's not a race. It's childhood.

Patience, or discipline?

"I don't think I have the patience to keep homeschooling."

Did you have the patience to teach your child how to walk? Did you have the patience to teach them to hold a spoon? Did you have the patience to teach them to ride a bike? Did you have the patience to teach them how to play a board game? Did you have the patience to teach them how to swing? Did you have the patience to teach them everything they learned before kindergarten?

We always find a way to do what we want most. If your kids learned to walk and talk and eat and play and dress themselves under your care, they can learn to read and write and add and think under your care, too.

If you think you can't do it, you have bought the lie that only experts can teach children academics. If you can parent, you can teach. It's all the same.

Have you taught your children to obey you? Have you taught them the God-ordained order of the family? Have you taught them to come when called, to obey quickly and cheerfully, to not argue or talk back, and to respect your authority?

I believe that what we call a lack of patience is actually a lack of discipline -- in ourselves and in our children. It takes work and self-sacrifice to consistently train children, daily and throughout their childhood. It takes dependence on God's plan and His promises, knowing that both we and our children will reap great rewards.

Flip that schedule

Sometimes our homeschooling is on the struggle bus, and we don't know exactly why, or what to do.

May I interest you in a new schedule?

Try adjusting your "school year" for a little while. This could be the easy adjustment that you needed.

Some examples:
- 4 school days a week
- 3 weeks on, 1 week off
- Earlier mornings
- Later mornings
- 2 heavy school days + 2 light days

The possibilities are pretty endless! Look at your whole calendar and tweak your school schedule to be more conducive to rest, work, ministry, and peace.

Have you tried a year-round school schedule?

Having a year-round school schedule means that whether it's July or March or December, we can have school 5 days a week or take a whole week off for deep cleaning or vacation.

We can adapt to Dad's work schedule.

We can drop everything when the weather is perfect.

We can cancel school and help a friend or family member.

We don't get behind when someone is sick.

Year-round school (for us) means that we have school 3-4 days per week, most of the time, but not all year round. We do have school in the summer (in Texas it's *not* nice outside), but we take almost the entire month of December off. If Dad is off work, or we want to get out and do something, we take off more days. We're not always doing school, but we're *consistently* doing school.

Being a home school family means that our calendar isn't dictated by anyone but us. It's just one thing on our long list of reasons for homeschooling.

We are a family, not a school.

Imperfect homeschooling

"We are living life, as imperfect and unplanned as it can be. Education is very important, but so is flexibility, independence, and maturity. On the days that I cannot be the mother that I want to be, my kids are learning and growing in ways that no textbook can teach. They are gaining their academic education during real-life circumstances."

In my book, *Anyone Can Homeschool*, I devoted an entire chapter to homeschooling with chronic illness. I share my story of living with migraines and how home education is managed. I also share the story of a mom with MS who homeschools her three kids.

There is no perfect life or home or family or homeschool. We are all doing what we can with what we have. That is what God asks of us, and it will not look like anyone else's family.

Our sacred burden

We say fun things and post cute memes about raising arrows and drinking coffee and wiping noses and giving all the glory to God.

But it's not just cute, it's real. James Dobson once said that "raising children is the most important job in the universe." It's hard and important all at the same time. Think about it: we are shaping the future when we put in the work to raise healthy, godly children. We are influencing the church, governments, and the culture for generations.

Some days are wonderful, and some days are a mess. Some days you wonder if anyone is listening to you.

"Mothers of young children, your work is most holy. You are fashioning the destinies of immortal souls. The powers folded up in the little ones that you hushed to sleep in your bosoms last night, are powers that shall exist forever. You are preparing them for their immortal destiny and influence. Be faithful. Take up your sacred burden reverently.

Be sure that your heart is pure and that your life is sweet and clean."

So drink that coffee! You're going to need it!

The obedience problem

Often times, homeschoolers feel exasperated by an unruly child and their first thought is, "I can't do this homeschooling thing." They decide that sending the child back to government school is the only answer.

Don't do that!

Parenting requires us to go all in, when it's hard and when it's pleasant. Turning over the hardest part of the day to a government school will not solve anything. In fact, it's quite the opposite.

If homeschooling is hard, it's not homeschooling that's the problem. If your child won't obey, you have an obedience problem. The solution is to teach and expect obedience. Yes, I know it sounds easier than it is, but it's possible and necessary.

Take the time to train your child. Stop the school lessons when disobedience and rebellion occur, and deal with it promptly. Gently remind your child of the expected behavior, discipline them when needed, and pray together. Maybe you will resume the school work, or maybe you will pick it up again tomorrow. But don't let an unruly child control the home. Bring peace and order, and the school work will eventually get back on track.

Training is Biblical

Obedience to parents is a theme repeated all throughout scripture. It is the one requirement specifically for children. Parents are admonished over and over again to train, love, and discipline their children.

It is not mean to train our children to obey. It is not toxic or abusive. Discipline is another word for training. Training is good.

God knows what makes for a happy home and a happy world; we need only to follow His Word.

"We have come to a turning point in the road. If we turn to the right mayhap our children and our children's children will go that way; but if we turn to the left, generations yet unborn will curse our names for having been unfaithful to God and to His Word." -Charles Spurgeon[x]

Titus 2 is for everyone

Dear mom, can we talk about planning for the future? Namely, our children's futures?

We hear from parents who don't think they can homeschool because they have two incomes, an expensive mortgage, and a lifestyle that's hard to give up. Knowing the sacrifices it takes to make homeschool our children, doesn't it make sense to teach our sons and daughters to avoid this dilemma in their future?

Let's encourage our sons and daughters to pursue a one-income lifestyle. Let's admonish our sons to seek careers that support a family well. Let's prepare our daughters to manage a home efficiently on one income. Let's counsel our sons and daughters in the fashion of Titus 2.

"But as for you, teach what accords with sound doctrine. Older men are to be sober-minded, dignified, self-controlled, sound in faith, in love, and in steadfastness. Older women likewise are to be reverent in behavior, not slanderers or slaves to much wine. Men are to be sober-minded, dignified,

self-controlled, sound in faith, in love, and in steadfastness. Older women likewise are to be reverent in behavior, not slanderers or slaves to much wine. They are to teach what is good, and so train the young women to love their husbands and children, to be self-controlled, pure, working at home, kind, and submissive to their own husbands, that the word of God may not be reviled. Likewise, urge the younger men to be self-controlled." (Titus 2: 1-6)

As moms and dads, *we* should be modeling Titus 2 to our children. We can encourage our sons to provide well for their families. We can train our daughters to be content as mothers at home. We can teach them to prepare well for their future and to choose their spouses wisely.

Knowing what we know now, let's teach our sons and daughters what we wish we'd known.

Families are not institutions

When my children were all at home, I used to make sure the kids got outside for a while everyday, even if it was cold. They got vitamin D from the sunshine. They got fresh air for their immune system. They got exercise for their growing bodies.

I didn't "call it PE" because we were not an institution. I called it play time because they were kids.

Sometimes they rode bikes, jumped on the trampoline, or played in the woods. Sometimes they mowed, or cleaned the chicken coop, or cleaned up the yard.

I didn't "call it home economics" because we were not an institution. I called it "doing their part" because we were a family.

Too often we want to fit every category of our normal life into the perfect "school subject slot." We want to feel like we measure up to the checklist of public schools.

Hey. Why did you choose not to use the public schools?

Don't imitate. Don't replicate. You are free from those arbitrary slots. Don't try to squeeze your family back into them. Let kids be kids. Let them play, learn, and grow without labeling every activity.

An unspeakable privilege

"A mother is a chalice, the vessel without which no human being has ever been born. She is created to be a life-bearer, cooperating with her husband and with God in the making of a child. What a solemn responsibility. What an unspeakable privilege--a vessel divinely prepared for the Master's use."

~ Elisabeth Elliot[xi]

Laura Ingalls Wilder on motherhood

"What a wonderful power mothers have in their hands! They shape the lives of children today; through them the lives of the men and women of tomorrow, and through them the nations and the world."

- Laura Ingalls Wilder, *Little House in the Ozarks*

"And just as a little thread of gold, running through a fabric, brightens the whole garment, so women's work at home, while only the doing of little things, like the golden gleam of sunlight runs through and brightens all the fabric of civilization."

- Laura Ingalls Wilder, *Little House in the Ozarks*

"I believe it would be much better for everyone if children were given their start in education at home. No one understands a child as well as his mother, and children are so different that they need individual training and study. A teacher with a roomful of pupils cannot do this. At home, too, they are in their mother's care. She can keep them from learning immoral things from other children."

- Laura Ingalls Wilder, *Little House in the Ozarks*

Teaching your children a biblical worldview

Focus on the Family says, "A Biblical worldview is based on the infallible Word of God. When you believe the Bible is entirely true, then you allow it to be the foundation of everything you say and do."

I grew up homeschooled from the age of 11. Without even thinking about the word "worldview," my mom made a Biblical worldview a part of our daily lessons. How?

Scripture memory.

Every month we memorized a new chapter or portion of a chapter of the Bible. We also memorized single verses at different times.

Those memorized scriptures are still with me today. And they have absolutely formed my Biblical worldview. Whether I encounter fear, failure, hard decisions, moral dilemmas, whether it's my philosophy, my Christianity, my parenting, or my conversations, multiple scriptures come back to me in the midst of circumstances.

We didn't have a worldview curriculum. I don't have an organized database of scriptures for certain situations. It's the Holy Spirit that prompts these reminders when I need them, because the Scriptures are already in my head.

Mothers, don't fret over the perfect Bible curriculum, or whether your child attends Awanas or Bible Bowl, or whether you've got a Worldview class scheduled for high school. Teach your children to hide God's Word in their hearts. It will serve them well the rest of their lives.

*"Thy word is a lamp to my feet and a light to my path." (*Psalm 119:105)

Training is a marathon

Training children is not a one-and-done thing. It's not achieved with a chore chart. It's not consequences for bad behavior. It's not a list of rules. It's not lofty expectations.

It's all of these things combined, repeatedly. Yearly, daily, hourly training. It's teaching and training, talking and modeling, reviewing and reminding.

Training is a long-term assignment. Just as with a fruit tree, the fruit is something you wait patiently for, but if you plant, fertilize, water, and prune consistently, the fruit will come. It will be worth the work and the wait.

Children are the same. We have to invest our time, lots of time, and wait on the Lord. We teach, train, talk, love, and do it all over again. Some kids soak it up and show fruit early, while others require more training over time.

Don't get discouraged when you say the same thing every day for what seems like eternity. And don't expect to have a new kid by Friday.

Teach and train with love and patience. It will be worth it.

Play the long game

Elections won't change our nation. Raising godly children definitely will.

Yes, it's very important to vote and to make an educated choice when doing so. It's a privilege that Americans have, and it should not be ignored.

But do you know what's even more effective? Raising a whole bunch of future voters who can think logically, biblically, and who are not educated by the government school system.

When you have many children, they will grow up and become members of a society that needs them to be well-educated and prepared for such responsibility.

Voting in elections is what we do in the present; raising godly children who will vote (and maybe run) in elections for years into the future is the long game. The Marxists in government education are playing the long game; are you?

Physical activity is free

Dear homeschool mamas, don't fret about P.E. courses for your children. Don't feel pressure to sign them up for sixteen different activities a week. Physical Education is a public school thing. YOU are not a public school.

Kids do need physical activity, and it comes naturally to them. Haven't you noticed how much they wiggle in a chair? They WANT to be active.

Send them outside to run races, throw a ball, climb a tree, chase butterflies, dig holes, build forts, and play pretend.

Get some friends together for a game of basketball, volleyball, or kickball. Challenge them to do a certain number of push-ups or jumping jacks. Meet friends at the park. Take breaks between reading sessions for a walk in the neighborhood.

Organized sports and paid lessons are fun. And they are also *extra*. Don't worry if everyone else is doing them. Everyone else doesn't have your budget, your schedule, or your kids.

Consider family time. Do organized sports and lessons reduce the amount of time the children spend with Dad? Do they keep you running to lessons several days per week? Do they take precedence over family meal times? Are the little ones living in their car seats?

Good old-fashioned play and sunshine are free, and are really all your children need. Free yourself and let those kids loose!

Training children for heaven

"A true Christian must be no slave to fashion, if he would train his child for heaven. He must not be content to do things merely because they are the custom of the world; to teach them and instruct them in certain ways, merely because it is usual; to allow them to read books of a questionable sort, merely because everybody else reads them; to let them form habits of a doubtful tendency, merely because they are the habits of the day.

He must train with an eye to his children's souls. He must not be ashamed to hear his training called singular and strange. What if it is? The time is short–the fashion of this world passeth away. He that has trained his children for heaven, rather than for earth–for God rather than for man–he is the parent that will be called wise at the last." –J.C. Ryle[xii]

Don't imitate the world's education

"Homeschoolers could slowly be changing the culture of education all over the world. Instead, it is the other way round: Homeschoolers are defaulting to imitating the world's educational culture.

Why? Because we are afraid and fear causes us to do things that, while relieving our fears, harm our children's futures which is exactly what public school does to its children.

If you have been paying even minimal attention, you would know that the public school's way of educating children (meaning its curriculum choices and the way that curricula is taught) is under a microscope and is being largely discredited. Yet, the fear under which most homeschoolers live causes them to default to teaching the same subjects that are taught in the public schools and in the same way those subjects are taught.

Even if it takes another generation, homeschoolers eventually must be willing to do something else, or we can simply add homeschooling to public schooling, private schooling, and Christian schooling as alternative means of replicating public schooling's failed educational philosophies."

—Chris Davis, *Gifted: Raising Children Intentionally*[xiii]

Bible, reading, and math

On "non-school-days" my kids know that they still have a short list of requirements: Bible, reading, and math.

Why?

First, if we don't have plans to go somewhere, a little productivity of the mind is a good thing. They still have a mostly free day to do things they want, but I want to develop the habit of industry.

Second, daily Bible reading and study is learned through habit. If I make it a priority, they will, too.

Third, reading everyday builds literate minds without any other lessons. They fill their minds with beautiful language, literature, history or science, and always — a good story.

Finally, math is one of those things that is best learned without interruption. A long summer break requires tons of review, but math lessons three or four times a week keep the momentum going (and honestly? It prevents mush-brain).

This threesome usually takes about an hour or hour and a half. For a "non-school-day" that's just enough to engage their minds and still allow plenty of free time.

Does this count?

If you're tempted to "count" a walk around the neighborhood as P.E., let it go.

If you're tempted to "count" a grocery store trip as home economics, let it go.

If you're tempted to "count" planting seeds as science, let it go.

If you're tempted to "count" a visit to a museum as history, let it go.

Counting everything your kids do so that you can impress some bureaucrat somewhere is one of the fastest ways to cause homeschool stress and burnout.

Let your daughter enjoy that walk. Let your son enjoy the WW2 display. Let them bake cookies without turning it into a lesson.

It doesn't have to go on a checklist for you to know it's making them think. But what's more, life isn't all school subjects. It's family time, laughing, working, thinking, and being well-rounded. "Counting" something is for education bureaucrats. Learning is real life.

Continue the race

"Therefore, strengthen the hands which hang down, and the feeble knees, and make straight paths for your feet, so that what is lame may not be dislocated, but rather be healed." (Hebrews 12:12-13 NKJV)

John MacArthur expands on these verses: "The author returns to the race metaphor begun in vv.1-3 and incorporates language taken from Isaiah 35:3 to describe the disciplined individual's condition like a weary runner whose arms drop and knees wobble. When experiencing trials in his life, the believer must not allow the circumstances to get the best of him. Instead, he must endure and get his second wind so as to be renewed to continue the race."[xiv]

How?

Prayer, rest, Bible study, thankfulness, and worship, usually in that order.

Why?

Have you ever put into words why you're homeschooling?

You could probably rattle off a couple of reasons, but when you put pen to paper (or finger to screen, ahem), it makes you think more deeply about this journey of discipling your children.

Writing it down inspires you to ponder more than "secular public schools" or "better education."

I encourage you and your husband to mull this over. Take a week or two to jot down all of the reasons that come to mind. Put them into sentences or paragraphs. Create a vision statement for your homeschool.

Oh, and leave room to add to it.

If you can't think of any reasons, read your Bible and watch the news!

Write it out, type it up, and keep it handy. When days are hard, or impossible, consult your vision statement. You'll realize it's not impossible, and even when it's hard, it's so worth it.

Dear homeschooling mama,

Don't let the pressure of the world around you bring unneeded stress into your home this year. Don't let the educational goals of others dictate what happens in your home.

Assess each of your children individually: what are your goals for them? What are their talents and gifts? Do they need more work or encouragement to reach these goals? Do they need free time and rest to explore their gifts?

Assess the vision you and your husband have for the family; are you keeping this long-term vision in mind with your daily routine? Is it being pushed aside to make time for what others deem important?

Maybe you have a child struggling in math, and you suddenly feel "behind." Remember, you don't have to stall or repeat an entire grade for the sake of one subject. Take a couple of days each week to patiently review and drill.

Maybe you see other families on a strict school schedule, and you wonder if you're slacking because you need a break. Don't worry about what everyone else is doing; you know what your family needs! Embrace the break and spend some down time making memories!

Is everyone else using a popular curriculum, and it doesn't work for your family? Great! You are not them! Choose and use what your children need. Buy what fits your budget. Implement the courses that fit your life.

Remember the big picture! God gave you these children. Part of your purpose is to direct their education. But God also wants us to love them, train them, shelter them, and disciple them.

Ask God what the vision for your family should be, and how to accomplish that. Seek His direction for all aspects of your family's lives. And then rest in the knowledge that what God has for your family is much different than what He has for everyone else, *"casting all your care upon Him, for He cares for you."* (1 Peter 5:7 NKJV)

References

[i] *Charlotte Mason (2013). "The Original Home School Series", p.103, Simon and Schuster*

[ii] L Carroll Judson, (1838) *"Able and Mighty Men,"* published 2021 by Nicki Truesdell

[iii] J. C. Ryle (1888) *The Duties of Parents*, published by Wm. Hunt & Co.

[iv] J. R. Miller (1882). "The Parent's Part," https://www.gracegems.org/Miller/parents_part.htm

[v] John Taylor Gatto (2009), Weapons of Mass Instruction, New Society Publishers

[vi] Josh Niemi (2017), Expository Parenting, published by Josh Niemi

[vii] Nancy Leigh Demoss (2013), Revive Our Hearts podcast https://www.reviveourhearts.com/podcast/revive-our-hearts/training-next-generation/

[viii] Israel Wayne (2017), *Education: Does God Have an Opinion?* Published by Master Books

[ix] Nicki Truesdell (2020), *Anyone Can Homeschool*, published by Nicki Truesdell

[x] Charles Spurgeon (1888), Holding Fast the Faith – Sermon, published in Metropolitan Tabernacle Pulpit Volume 34

[xi] Elisabeth Elliot (1992), "The Shaping of a Christian Family," published by Thomas Nelson, Inc.

[xii] Ibid., J. C. Ryle

[xiii] http://homeschoolingwisdom.com/part-2-why-we-are-not-yet-ready-to-do-something-else/

[xiv] John MacArthur (1997), *The MacArthur Study Bible*, published by Word Publishing.

Also from Nicki Truesdell

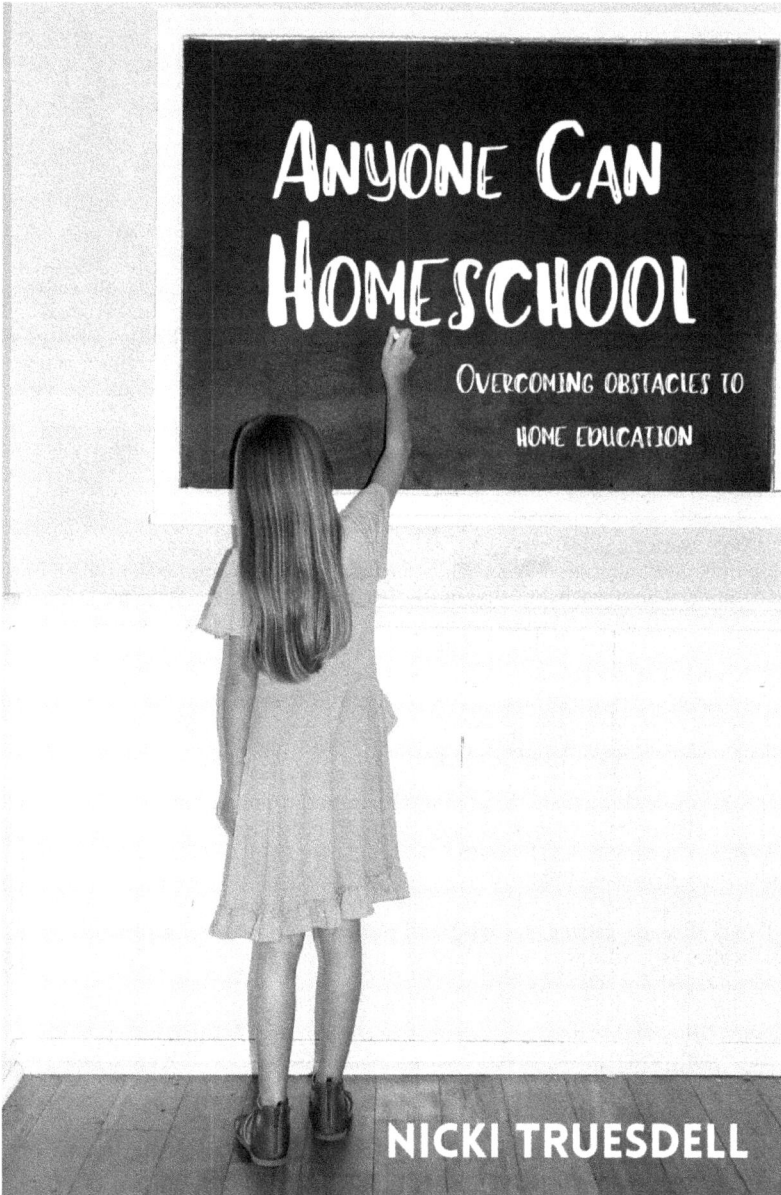

ANYONE CAN HOMESCHOOL

Overcoming obstacles to home education

NICKI TRUESDELL

Anyone Can Homeschool:
Overcoming Obstacles to Home Education

How to educate your children at home even under the most impossible circumstances.

Moms and dads, you have all that it takes to educate your children, whether your circumstances are ideal or not. Nicki Truesdell, blogger, mother of 5, and second-generation homeschooler, shares her stories of 20 years of home education through many ups and downs, and how she learned to adapt to every situation. In this book you will hear from real people who are doing it, even in the most difficult of circumstances:

- single parents
- grandparents
- families with chronic illness
- children with special needs
- working parents

...and many other situations. This book is the product of many discussions, both in real life and online, where frustrated and desperate parents expressed a desire to find an alternative to the public schools. Like so many, they automatically assumed that homeschooling was only for those families who had neatly organized lives, complete with a large income, a school room in their house, a college degree, and obedient children. A must-read for every parent who is desperate for an education solution.

This book includes two very important parts:

Part One begins with what we think education is, and what it actually is. This is followed by individual chapters devoted to specific circumstances (single parents, low income, etc.). Dig in to understanding education vs. *home education*, and how to apply these concepts to your personal life.

Part Two is all about getting started. You'll read about how to find your state homeschooling law, withdraw your children, set up your homeschool, choose curriculum, set a schedule, and much more.

Nicki truly believes that *anyone* can homeschool when they begin to understand education at its core. This book will open your eyes to the possibilities and help you get started right away.

Get *Anyone Can Homeschool* on Amazon, Audible, Kindle, and nickitruesdell.com

www.ingramcontent.com/pod-product-compliance
Lightning Source LLC
Chambersburg PA
CBHW071952100426
42736CB00043B/2829